SEVENTH
APOCALYPSE

The Unveiling of the Cornerstone for
the Islamic States of the Americas

JOHN ELLIS ISHMAEL BRIDGE BE

authorHOUSE®

AuthorHouse™
1663 Liberty Drive
Bloomington, IN 47403
www.authorhouse.com
Phone: 1 (800) 839-8640

Published by AuthorHouse   09/07/2016

ISBN: 978-1-5246-2597-9 (sc)
ISBN: 978-1-5246-2595-5 (hc)
ISBN: 978-1-5246-2596-2 (e)

Library of Congress Control Number: 2016913801

Print information available on the last page.

Any people depicted in stock imagery provided by Thinkstock are models, and such images are being used for illustrative purposes only. Certain stock imagery © Thinkstock.

This book is printed on acid-free paper.

Scripture quotations marked KJV are from the Holy Bible, King James Version (Authorized Version). First published in 1611. Quoted from the KJV Classic Reference Bible, Copyright © 1983 by The Zondervan Corporation.

Scripture quotations marked NIV are taken from the Holy Bible, New International Version®. NIV®. Copyright © 1973, 1978, 1984 by International Bible Society. Used by permission of Zondervan. All rights reserved. [Biblica]

Table of Contents

Dedication

Dedicated to the Ancestors and Descendants of those who
dedicate themselves to enjoying and promoting peace,
goodwill, social justice and spiritual enhancement.

Acknowledgement

I wish to acknowledge the following newspapers and their editors who chose to share my opinions with their readership:

Sun Herald of South Mississippi

Natchez Democrat of Southwest Mississippi

Franklin Advocate of Southwest Mississippi

Clarion Ledger of Jackson, Mississippi

Morning News Tribune of Tacoma, Washington

Denver Post/ Rocky Mountain News of Denver/Aurora, Colorado

Northwest Guardian of Fort Lewis, Washington

Herald Post of El Paso, Texas

Stars and Stripes of U.S Army Europe

Introduction

Peace and goodwill.

I bear witness that there is no other God but God and that Creation is the messenger of God.

I bear witness that the charity of doing for others as we want done for us is beneficial.

I bear witness that prayer, meditation, reflection, contemplation and seclusion are beneficial.

I bear witness that fasting, whether for the body or behavior, is beneficial.

I bear witness that the Universe is the Sacred House of Prayer and Worship.

I bear witness that fighting oppression, aggression, ignorance and narcissism is beneficial.

I bear witness that the freedom to be an individual promoting peace and goodwill is beneficial.

Seeking to glorify and obey God, our Creator and Sustainer, the Most Loving, Most Gracious, Most Just, Most Free One, (Exodus 3:14; John 12:28; Quran 20:8) I greet you with respect and humility.

The positive progress of the human spirit toward establishing a more interconnected, just and caring society has brought humanity to a new dawn and many are awakening with a refreshed and rejuvenated relationship with themselves, each other, the Creation and our Creator.

Like its wicked twin, institutional racism, institutional religion is being exposed for its fraud, fallacy, fantasy, hypocrisy, vanity and ungodliness. Current and recent events are allowing humans to distinguish between fraud and genuine, fallacy and fact, fantasy and faith, hypocrisy and sincerity, vanity and service and ungodliness and submission to God's omnipotent will and design.

Humans who seek to enjoy a harmonious relationship with themselves, each other, the Creation and our Creator are gradually reclaiming our divine birthright to observe the laws and lessons of Creation and enjoy the Creator's seven gifts of freedom, love, truth, justice, hope, compassion and life.

During this spiritual metamorphosis it is becoming more apparent that the ungodly, pretentious, "pious fraud" being committed by most institutional religions and their followers who aid and abet the blasphemous fraud, is, wittingly or unwittingly, an evil effort to hinder humanity from enjoying its divine birthright.

Wherever the fraud, fallacy, fantasy, hypocrisy, vanity and ungodliness within institutional religion is being displayed, the spirituality, mentality and technology of our time are causing more humans to be able to distinguish between the fraud and blasphemy of institutional religion and the simple and authentic path which leads to harmony within relationships.

Islam (an AfroArab word that means "at peace with the will of God" and "submission to the will of God") is the fastest growing faith in the Americas and is on a trajectory to be the way of life for the majority of the inhabitants of the western hemisphere who seek a genuine, sincere and harmonious relationship with themselves, each other, Creation and our Creator.

As current and recent events in the Middle East expose the fraud, fallacy, fantasy, hypocrisy, vanity and ungodliness of those who have attempted during the past 1300 years to institutionalize, redefine, paganize, Arabize and codify the simple and authentic message and method of submission to the will of God (Islam), it is appropriate and a blessing that the simple and authentic message and method of Islam is being proclaimed, protected and projected in the Americas (aka, Amiracle; aka, Atchyzlan; aka Western Hemisphere; Quran 47:38).

Freeing Islam from those who attempted to institutionalize it and proclaiming that the simple and authentic way for all humans to submit to the will of God is to (1) obey the laws and lessons of Creation and, exercising the application of dignity and reason, (2) enjoy the seven gifts of our divine birthright, hopefully the message of this little book will be beneficial in helping humanity in the further construction and maintenance of a better society.

This compilation of published letters, poems, warnings and recommendations shared during the past forty years is intended to proclaim and prepare the way for the coming of ISA (Islamic States of the Americas) and serve as a unifying factor for Believers/Behavers of the future.

Just as Islam is on the ascendancy in the West and undergoing a reevaluation in the East, Christianity and Judaism, in the East and West, are in their decline and are on a trajectory to being an irrelevant, superficial, obsolete or dead replica of institutional religion.

The idolatrous Judeo-Christian mythology, theology and dogma that have betrayed the Islamic monotheistic message and method of the original Akhenaten-Hagar-Abraham-Akan Hebrews are being reevaluated in the West and that reevaluation may yet divert Judeo-Christianity from its current trajectory and return it to its original Islamic roots and principles.

It is with this fact in mind that I share this segment of the first part of Thomas Paine's "Age of Reason" as part of this introduction or opening to the observations, recommendations and warnings of Seventh Apocalypse: The unveiling of the cornerstone for the Islamic States of the Americas.

The Age of Reason

by Thomas Paine

"TO MY FELLOW-CITIZENS OF THE
UNITED STATES OF AMERICA:

I PUT the following work under your protection. It contains my opinions upon Religion. You will do me the justice to remember, that I have always strenuously supported the Right of every Man to his own opinion, however different that opinion might be to mine. He who denies to another this right, makes a slave of himself to his present opinion, because he precludes himself the right of changing it.

The most formidable weapon against errors of every kind is Reason. I have never used any other, and I trust I never shall.

Your affectionate friend and fellow-citizen,

THOMAS PAINE

Luxembourg, 8th Pluvoise,
Second Year of the French Republic, one and indivisible.
January 27, O. S. 1794.

PART FIRST.

Soon after I had published the pamphlet Common Sense, in America, I saw the exceeding probability that a revolution in the system of government would be followed by a revolution in the system of religion.......

Human inventions and priestcraft would be detected; and man would return to the pure, unmixed and unadulterated belief of one God, and no more."

SEVENTH
APOCALYPSE

The Unveiling of the Cornerstone for
the Islamic States of the Americas

JOHN ELLIS ISHMAEL BRIDGE BE

Poem # 1

A WIND OF CHANGE

There's a wind of change stirring in the West:
An air of reconsideration; an air of re-examination at best.
There's a wind of change stirring in the West.

Standing on the rock or standing on the sand,
Will the shout be due to humiliation?
Or jubilation across the land?

Build a society on the sand or build a society on the rock.
Is it a society from which many will flee or
Is it a society to which many will flock?

There's a wind of change stirring in the West;
A whirling, howling and powerful wind,
Determined to put humanity to a test.

There's a wind of change stirring in the West;
Prepare and watch as it scatters or collects.
There's a wind of change stirring in the West.

There's a wind of change stirring in the West;
A gust of destruction at worse; a breeze of rebirth at best.
There's a wind of change stirring in the West.

Poem # 2

REVOLUTION

Revolution: Let the word freely flow
Revolution: Just how far are you prepared to go?

{Part 1}
White racism, Brown racism, Black racism- It's all the same game;
Played by those who hide behind a sheet of self-shame.
Burn that cross, Burn that scalp, Stereotype or hate, obey the KKK creed!
After all, who believes that fairytale about everyone being from Adam's seed?
What is she doing with that white boy? Why is she going with that black guy?
What is he doing with that Asian lady? Why is he going with that white girl?
White, brown and black members of the KKK ask, trapped in their tiny
world.

{Part 2}
Wearing Afros, Dreadlocks, Dashikis, Big Loop Earrings, FUBU and a
crucifix,
Many find themselves caught in an Ironic Twist
Where they protest about the evils and burdens of the white man
While they praise, worship, sing and shout and wait
For a straight-hair, whiteface savior to take them to the "promised land".
The ancestors must be turning in their graves, wondering how can it be?
That most of their descendants have rejected the Living God who heard
The ancestors' prayers during the Middle Passage over the sea.
The ancestors must be shaking their heads in disbelief
To see most of their descendants praising and believing in the same Cross
As those who stole, bought, sold and exported them to the "land of the Free".
Wearing Afros, Dreadlocks, Dashikis, Big Loop Earrings, FUBU and a
crucifix,
The worshippers of the Golden Calf find themselves in an Ironic Twist.

{Part 3}
Whether White, Black or Brown, rich, poor and middle-class slaves too

Sell their soul to Massa Gold to buy the same old thing that's labeled new.
The black, brown and white slaves of today are dependable, easy to Control.
In suit and tie, heels and pearls, shirt and jeans or uniforms, each bow
In the name of almighty Gold.
Car, house, habit, jewelry, shopping, shopping, shopping for that brand-name bling-bling
The modern day slaves of Massa Gold, to please the massa, will do anything.
Let Daycare raise the children, may the massa's will be done, sunrise to sunset.
With a little overtime or a second job, buy the kid a toy, yourself a Corvette.

{Part 4}
They offer you the flag, the anthem, the vote and a job and call it Democracy.
They offer you 90 days same as cash, 13% usury, 401k, MTV, CNN, BET, a police state and mandatory insurance and tell you, "You are Free!"
However, who owns the land, who owns the water, who owns the oil, who owns the electricity, who owns the politicians seeking your vote:
Seeking to represent you on this leaky, sinking boat.
"Go to the polls; get out and vote; exercise your rights", they all say-
Vote for your favorite stranger who will make more laws to take your money, your dignity and your freedom away.

{Part 5}
One woman says "$100 an hour; see you next week".
One woman says, "If I cook, clean and spread like smooth Jiffy, Maybe he'll be my man, give me a ring and make me complete".
Sex for sale, sex for fun, sex for free, sex for attention, sex to pay the bills, respectfully.
One man says "Here's the cash, see you next week".
One man says, "if I take her to dinner, buy her a mood ring and pay her rent, Maybe she'll be my woman and lick my feet'..
Sex for sale, sex for fun, sex for free, sex for gratitude, sex to pay the bills, respectfully!

{Part 6}
Some Christians say God has a mother and God died for all sins.
Some Christians say Jesus is God and the son of God,
sort of like strange Siamese Twins!
Some Jews say they are God's "chosen ones",
sort of like the teacher's pet

that's favored above all the rest!
Some Muslims, rejecting the Universe as the "Sacred House of Prayer"
say they must in unison pray facing Mecca as a holy site
as long as the one praying beside them isn't Sunni or isn't Shiite.
Some Buddhists say why worry, why be concerned, there is no God,
only Me!
Some Hindus say many gods are better than one,
sort of like Equal Opportunity!
Some Atheists say if God, like the wind, can't be seen,
how can one truly know?
Some Satanists say love and compassion is inhumane
and hate and vanity is the way to go.

{Part 7}
The door is opening, leading to a new day.
The door is opening, offering a new way.
The door is opening and those with eyes see the light.
The door is opening for those unafraid to fight.
The door is opening for those who dare to ask why?
The door is opening, inviting you to the Society of the OPEN SKY

Revolution: Just how far are you prepared to go?
Revolution: Let the word freely flow.
Revolution!

Letter # 1

22 Buffalo 6B1991 (Sep 1984)

Malpractice in the Pulpit

I am writing concerning malpractice in the pulpit.

This is a warning and a salutation to those who are true believers and seek to be true behavers but who have chosen to remain in the ritualistic, traditional atmosphere of organized, institutional religion.

Continue to walk in the way of those who believe in the One True One and continue to believe and behave in the true guidance offered by I AM (Exodus 3:14).

Observe and follow the words and teachings of the true Christ.

May you be able to distinguish between the words and ways of I AM and the words and ways of ritualistic religion.

There are many preachers, priests, imams, maharajas, popes and rabbis who have been placed by others and by themselves as pretenders to the throne.

"You will know them by their fruit".

It would be best if you at this time remove yourselves from false, ungodly religious institutions and gather yourselves, your children and other loved ones into the society of the open sky and enjoy Obedience to I AM.

If you choose to remain within the confines of organized religion then speak out and try to correct that which presents itself incorrectly.

El Paso, Texas

Letter # 2

Restoration Day 6B1992 (Easter 1985)
(Excerpt broadcasted on CBS "60 Minutes)

Re: Your Program on Palm Sunday about U.S. Paulists

Your program on Palm Sunday about the Pseudo-Christians, Paul, original sin, the trinity, bigotry and intolerance was a great example of how many Paulists continue to display the mark of misbelief on their forehead, as evidenced by the thoughts they think, and on their hand, as evidenced by the deeds they do. If Christ never taught the doctrine of original sin (Matt. 18:1-7) or the trinity (Deut. *6:4;* Mark 12:29-31; John 7:16-18; Quran 5:67-77] while Paul blatantly taught both, then are most Americans Paulists or Christians?

If Christ says he was sent by God to bring the truth into the world (John 18:37) in order to guide his brothers and sisters out of the wilderness of sin (Matthew 7:21-29), then why do Paulists betray Christ by proclaiming Jesus to be a god (Phillipians 2:5-8) or a scapegoat or blood-sacrifice whose only purpose was to die for their sins? (2 Corinth. 5:15-21; Hebrews 7:1-27).

Did Jesus die for the sins of the past, sins of the present or sins of the future? If Jesus died for the sins of the past, then who is responsible for the sins of the present and the future? (Matthew 12:31-33)

If Jesus died for the sins of the future then does that mean all sins are forgiven and therefore the whole notion of sin is moot?

Doesn't the doctrine of original sin insinuates that if a child dies without being baptized or accepting *Jesus* as her or his savior then that child dies in a state of inherited sin and is condemned to hell?

Doesn't the doctrine of the trinity insinuates that if Jesus is God, then God died for two days and nights, Jesus prayed to himself (John 12:28-30), Jesus sits at the right side of himself (Mark 16:19), Jesus raised himself from the dead and it is also redundant to "go through *Jesus* to get to God"?

As the world wades deeper into the baptismal fires of the Soul War, perhaps the time has come for many to decide whether they are followers of Christ (John 14:23-31; 20:16-18) or followers of Paul (1Tim. 2:11-12; 6:1-6).

Considering the vast number of citizens who follow Paul instead of Christ, I wonder whether it would be a misnomer to label America and the West as a Pseudeo-Christian society instead of a Judeo-Christian society.

Please allow me to answer your question about what would Jesus say if he observed the characters in your story about the Paulist.

Jesus would probably say: "Forgive them, for they know not what they do" or do they?

Aurora, Colorado

Letter # 3

Author gave bigoted view of Islam

It appears that in an attempt to head off this "war between the spirits," the media are desperately digging themselves deeper with their vile lies and absurdities against Islam, against the children of Earth and against the Most Gracious and Most Merciful One.

In the Aug. 7 Commentary,... having fallen under the illusion of religious bigotry and ignorance, stated in his last paragraph: "Iran's efforts will be rewarded if the United States mistake Iran for Islam and loses its resolve for fear of provoking an apocalyptic war with Islam. Ayatollah Khomeini cannot order such a war. His bluff must be called."

Well,.... is right by virtue of being wrong. Imam Khomeini has not ordered this war between the spirits (a war that began in 1957). The United States, by its present anti-Christ nature, will, as.... said, "call the bluff" and, as we say, receive its baptism – for the rejuvenation of those Americans with good hearts but deceived souls, for the destruction of those Americans with racist, materialistic, narcissistic hearts and third-mortgaged souls.

The United States did not, Iran did not, provoke the war between the spirits, but unrepentant racism, narcissism and materialism did.

Democratic capitalism and communist socialism, fueled by imperialism and slavery, did.

False Christians, false Jews, false Muslims, false polytheists, false atheists, false Satanists, false patriotism, false pride and hypocrisy did.

Denver/Aurora, Colorado

Letter # **4**

4 Fire 6B1997 (Jan 1990)

The Soul War

As the new year proceeds into history I wish to offer the following events to be observed in the days ahead.

The Cold War will continue to thaw and like a magnificent, giant mammoth awakened from its icy sleep, the world will find itself taking up it's weapons of sword, truth, faith, logic, revelation and love and going forth into the battles of the Soul War.

Consider this explanation of the Soul War.

Just as the people of the Eastern bloc rose up, not so much against socialism, but against corruption, so shall the people of the Western bloc rise up, not so much against capitalism, but against corruption. The people of the East and West and their reluctant allies will then realize, sometime around the Harvest Moon of 6B2001 (AD1994) that they've exchanged one form of corruption, namely deception, for its' brother, namely materialism. When the people of the East and West and their subject allies see where their quest for materialism has taken them, too late, they will realize that materialism feeds on narcissism and eventually drinks at the bloody fountain of racism.

In an attempt to appease the discontent and public disorder of civil disobedience brought about by narcissism, racism and the unequal acquisition of "stuff," the leaders of the northern hemisphere and their southern hemispheric allies shall direct the energy of the people of the Unholy Lok (a reference to Loki and Norse mythology) against Islam.

Those who call themselves Muslims, but are not, because they have added to and subtracted from the Quran as revealed to the Prophet and, in direct disobedience to the Quran (42: 13; 30: 31-32; 43: 64-65) divided themselves into sects by chasing after their formalism, ritualism, culture, hearsay and tradition shall, along with those who call themselves Abraham's children, but are not (Deuteronomy 28; 15; John 8: 39-45; Revelation 2: 9), sign the Unholiest of Unholy Pact with the followers of Loki and betray the Prophet, whose message shall be protected by the Miracles from inside Amiracle (aka, the western hemisphere; aka, the Americas; aka, Atchyzlan)

Who shall the Believer fear?

Thus the years ahead shall witness the long awaited birth of the Soul War.

The next nine years shall be as the ninth month of pregnancy for the Earth as the Birth of the New Dawn spring forth after the powerful contractions of the War Between the Spirits: the War Between Islam and the enemies of Islam, the Soul War.

Do not read this as a dark prophecy but read it as a prophecy of light, giving ample warning to the enemies of Islam and a joyous greeting to the Believers/Behavers.

From the Society of the Open Sky, welcome to our destiny and beyond.
May the Love of I Am guide us.
So be it.

Weisendorf, Germany

Letter # 5

Heart of the Muslim

In regard to the writers who are apparently unaware that the same one who created faith created logic. Third-grade math taught us the distinction between less than, equal to and greater than. The Gospel – according to John 14:28 – records the anointed messenger as saying, "My Father is greater than I." Perhaps these writers should let their theology refrain from mesmerizing them.

Islam, translated, means submission to the will of God (I AM, Allah, Jehovah, Jah, Great Spirit or whichever name a particular culture recognizes as the supreme existence). Miracle Muslims recognize I AM.

Muslim, translated, means any entity, individual or any aspect of Creation which submits to the will of the Supreme Existence – without adding partners.

The will of the Supreme Existence, interpreted by Muslims, is manifested in the laws and lessons of Creation and the experiences of love, forgiveness, faith, freedom, charity and the abolition of idolatry and oppression.

Muslims, historically and futuristically, feel all the true messengers, prophets, prophetesses and elements of existence (the sun, the seasons, the wind, the planets, the atom, the egg amd all of Creation) obediently submit to the will of the Supreme Existence.

Muslims do not differentiate (Quran 2: 136) between Moses, Jesus, Mohammed, Sitting Bull, Wovoka, Nat Turner or any messenger and feel that the worship of any messenger is blasphemy and goes against the will of the Supreme Existence and in essence is betraying the spirit of prophecy.

Racism, sexism, materialism, narcissism and false religion are considered to be the modern day idols of those who choose not to submit to the will of I AM.

As Islam becomes more a part of the modern world, I hope this statement can give an inside view of the core of the heart of the Muslim. After reading this, perhaps quite a few individuals will awaken to find the old saying, "all children are born Muslim but some become victims of beastheology," a saying of unnecessary buts. Let all children continue to submit to the will and love of I AM.

Nurnburg/Furth, Germany

Letter # 6

Religion and the armed forces

If the U.S. courts have ruled it is illegal to support, enhance or discriminate or establish religion in public schools or any public-funded entity; if the U.S. Constitution warns against and forcefully forbids the establishment of or discrimination against religion; and if the U.S. armed forces are public funded, then is there the slightest possibility that Army Reg 165-1 is anti-Constitutional in its insistence to establish religion or at least promote a particular religion based on majority bias and bigotry?

... As Miracle Muslims can my children expect a week or two out of school during the Festival of Fasting in spring just like children of other religions can expect days out of school during Christmas?

... Does this mean that just like AFRTS gives airing to one particular religious view, it can be expected to give a percentage of air time to other faiths or beliefs?

If AR 165-1 is based on percentage representation of the community and if AFRTS, DODDs schools, bookstores, chaplaincy and the armed forces in general are genuinely convinced of the legality and justice of implementing this regulation, then should my family, representing approximately 0.7777777 percent of the community, expect our "legal" share of respect?

Thanks for your effort to allow us an opportunity to seek an avenue of consideration of our status as Miracle Muslims.

Nürnberg, Germany

Letter # 7

21 Buffalo 6B1998 (Sep 1991)

'Constitutional bigotry'

I am writing in reference to those who have written recently ridiculing those offended by prayers at military functions.

Col. executive director of Armed Forces Chaplain's Board,?? recent answer to a question in your Readers' Action Line concerning AR 165-1, actually admitted that the chaplaincy service is "constitutional" because it supports "the free exercise of religion." As a constitutional patriot I feel any time the words "support" and "religion" appears together in an attempt to justify public-funded religious practices then I view such explanations as either constitutional bigotry, ignorance or hypocrisy.

Col. also admitted that Christmas is "legally" observed in public schools and other public institutions because it is no longer a religious holiday but is now a secular holiday.

Such an admission of the government's audacity to sidestep the Constitution by secularizing a religious holiday should be alarming, as well as offensive, to all citizens – especially Christians, not to mention non-believers.

After all, at what point or with what explanation will the chaplaincy permit or deny Satanist chaplains to provide "invocations" at military functions or on the occasion of troop deployments? Should Satanists expect a chaplain for their group also?

Once again, the question is not whether an atheist, agnostic, Muslim, Christian, Jew, Jehovah's Witness, Mormon, Buddhist, Wiccan, New Ager or whatever has the right to sit, stand or be excused during a prayer but whether such an invocation is anti-constitutionally offensive to the particular minority in the audience.

Remember, the U.S. Constitution and its foundation, the Bill of Rights, are designed to protect the minority from the majority.

Nürnberg, Germany

Letter # 8

Constitutional basis

A recent letter sought to "put aright: 'Remember, the Constitution and its foundation, the Bill of Rights, are designed to protect the minority from the majority'" in reply to a letter about religion in the military.

If the Bill of Rights is not the' foundation of the U.S. Constitution then I challenge anyone to remove the Bill of Rights and see if the US Constitution will sink into mud or stand steady 200 years from 1991.

Were the landowning, educated, pursuers of property such as Jefferson, Paine, Banneker or other founding fellas of the minority or majority among the British colonists?

Was taxation without representation more a burden on the uneducated, landless, property-less majority of British subjects or on the plantation owners, merchants and clergy minority?

The abolition of slavery and the inclusion of women, as well as the miraculous survival of the people (the original and inalienable landowners), should provide an example of protection "from the majority," as Article 5 of the Constitution envisioned.

Perhaps those who feel freedom of expression "is dangerous, untrue and must not be tolerated" would feel less threatened if, instead of seeing the word "foundation," they could read between the lines and see the word sub-conscience.

Nurnburg, Germany

Letter # 9

21 Soil Seed 6B1999 (Mar 1992)

New leaders, please respect 1ˢᵗ Amendment

As a sympathizer and admirer of the GOP of Thaddeus Stevens and as a Miracle Muslim who is a descendant of the Cherokee, African and European, I wish to congratulate Gov. _ and Lt. Gov. for their historic opportunity to guide Mississippi into the next century with the will of I AM (Exodus 3:13-15).

However I hope the leaders of the state, the nation and the world will truly consider the wisdom offered in the First Amendment to the U.S. Constitution concerning the relationship between religion and government.

If Satanism is a religion, will today's leaders feel comfortable having a Satanist schoolteacher invoke a prayer at the beginning of their children's or grandchildren's school day? One person's god may be another person's demon. Islam means submission to the will of I AM (God, Creator, Jah, Jehovah, Great Spirit, Allah, Yahweh or whatever name a culture recognizes as the Supreme Existence).

A Muslim is an individual or entity which submits its personal will to the will of I AM (Matthew 12:48-50) without adding partners of worship; whether the partners are racism, sexism, materialism, narcissism, or a messenger or a saint.

Since the anointed messenger Jesus, in the gospel according to John 14:24-31, clarified his desire to completely submit to the will of I AM, then hopefully it will be understandable why Muslims, including Christ, find it offensive to pray to anyone or anything else beside I AM (Matthew 7:12-29). We believe all worship should be directed to I AM (Revelation 19:9-11) and that life is more pleasant when we submit to the will of I AM – a will inclusive of love, forgiveness, faith, freedom, charity and the abolition of oppression and idolatry.

I hope this letter will not offend the innocent, but I hope it will give a view worth seeing. Let all children remain in the embrace of the truth and love of I AM.

Biloxi, Mississippi

Letter # 10

21 Fish 6B1999 (June 1992)

Covenant and Constitution

I hope the leaders of the state, nation and world will truly consider the wisdom offered in the First Amendment to the U. S. Constitution concerning the relationship between religion and government.

If Satanism is a religion, will today's leaders feel comfortable having a Satanist schoolteacher invoke a prayer at the beginning or end of their children's or grandchildren's school day or school year? *Military chaplains take note*

As a Miracle Muslim who recognizes Christ as the anointed messenger but do not believe Christ is God (John:14:28 or John 20:17) my children and I find it offensive when some public speakers continue to spread lies, propaganda and misrepresentations about our brother and friend, Jesus. (Matthew 7:20-29).

I am pleased the Supreme Court's latest First Amendment decision recognizes the wisdom, freedom, tolerance and faith which the American Covenant (Constitution) offer to each of its citizens, regardless of and in spite of whichever religion a person chooses to show their allegiance to.

May each and every aspect of creation continue within the love, forgiveness, faith, freedom and charity offered by I AM. (Exodus 3:14)
Thank you,

Franklin County, Mississippi

Letter # 11

25 Wind 6B2000 (Feb 1993)

Muslims celebrate Ramadan

As the new moon appeared in the open sky this month, more than one billion Muslims began celebrating Ramadan – the month of fasting.

The Holy Quran (also known as the Koran) invites believers to fast in order to learn self-restraint and to celebrate the month in which the Holy Quran was sent to humanity as a guide distinguishing right from wrong.

Rejoicing over the miraculous gift of the Holy Quran, Muslims will fast during the daylight hours and read the Holy Quran while fellowshipping with their families and others.

Reading the entire Holy Quran during the month of Ramadan is a goal many Muslims try to accomplish. The rhythm, logic, faith and love expressed in the word revealed to Muhammad is embraced by believers as a foundation for justice, tolerance, deliverance, redemption and unity upon which all the children of creation may stand and enjoy the peace and blessings of God.

The Holy Quran will be read during the celebration of Ramadan as Muslims submit to the will of Allah (the Arabic word for God, which is used by Christian Arabs as well as by Muslim Arabs). Hopefully, the month of Ramadhan will be a time of reflection, self-observation and enlightenment for all the citizens of creation.

Muslims, who can be defined as believers who choose to submit to the will of God, believe the Holy Quran is a miracle in that it is the book which reveals the will of God concerning humanity's obligation to each other, to the rest of creation, and to God.

Islam, which means submission to the will of God, acknowledges the original Gospel (Matthew 12:48-50; John 20:17) and the original book given to the Children of Israel (Exodus 20:1-7) as being messages inviting humans to submit to the will of God and the Holy Qur-an also acknowledges many other messengers and nations to whom, by the mercy and grace of God, guidance has been offered.

The Holy Quran, Muslims believe, exists to clarify those issues which have divided believers, to invite and warn those who may be nonbelievers, or misbelievers and to confirm, with a greeting of peace, the message of love and truth which dwell in the heart of each child.

Although the original, clear message of the Holy Quran may have been blurred by the vanities and "isms" of adolescence, adulthood, culture, tradition, hearsay and sectarian or denominational theory or theology, the divine message will always be confirmed by the laws, lessons, truth and reason of Creation, the quintessential and original Word of God.

Ft Lewis, Tacoma, Washington

Letter # 12

26 Rain 6B2OO2 (Apr 1995)

Coverage reflected anti-Muslim bigotry

Thanks be to God, the media only had 48 hours in which to display their racist, un-American, pseudo Judeo-Christian bigotry against Muslims. Once again Muslims were presumed guilty until proven innocent.

As the investigation continues into the explosion despised around the world, I wonder if the media will refer to the suspects as Judeo-Christian fanatics?

As the Cold War continues to thaw and the world finds itself chin-deep in the baptismal fire of the Soul War, I urge the media to examine themselves and acknowledge the religious bigotry within their own editorial boards. Although the media apparently enjoy airing information about pseudo-Muslims there are many positive, true Muslim voices anxious to share in uplifting the message of love, compassion, freedom and justice. Perhaps the media should make more of an effort to allow all voices to be heard.

The Holy Quran teaches Muslims to live in peace within the fellowship of believers, yet be prepared to fight to defend the weak, oppressed, the disadvantaged, the poor, the children and the principles of justice. Muslims refuse to be pawns for any government, party, organization or any host of the many fashionable white-male-rage talk shows.

We invite all citizens to sincerely check out themselves and those they listen to and distinguish if what they see and hear are examples of true patriots or racist, bigoted patridiots.

Dupont, Washington

Warning # 1

REVOLUTION

Beware of the pretenders to the throne who claim to be what they are not as they seek, for their own selfish motives, to limit the freedom of other humans with their unreasonable and unnatural laws, rules, traditions, dogma and pseudo-ethics.

Beware of the imagination, the handiwork, the economic, psychological and social engineering, the elitist political and judicial systems, the blasphemous and hypocritical religions and all the isms concocted by the vanity, greed, shame, arrogance, ignorance, hatred and fear of some humans. Fueled by the greed, ignorance, complacency and fear of the Approval Junkies, the Control Freaks have apparently forgotten that there has been a great expanse of time when they didn't even exist and there will probably be an even greater expanse of time after they cease to exist in their fragile shell. They, the Approval Junkies and Control Freaks, fool only themselves as they pretend to be what they are not. If that is the path they choose, so be it. The rest of us choose to be Free People, seeking neither the approval nor disapproval of any human nor to control or be controlled by any human.

We the Free People, think, act, and react not out of fear of punishment or disapproval. We, the Free People, think, act and react not out of desire for reward or approval.
We, the Free People, think, act and react not out of a selfish motive to control others.
We, the Free People, think, act and react for no other motive than to promote social justice and spiritual enhancement in submission to God.
We, the Free People, choosing to live in submission only to the natural Law ordained by the Most Just Lawgiver, realize that freedom is the prerequisite for any human to be able to experience its God-given potential.

Beware of the pitfalls and snares of the Control Freaks and Approval Junkies who seek to distort and manipulate Eternal Truth in order to justify their selfish motives. You will see them using their scriptures, their constitutions, their ethics and their conscience to cover the injustice they do against themselves and others.

Eternal Truth and transitory truth are but two of the many voices standing along the corridor of Life calling out to Humanity. If the transitory truth is supported by the Eternal Truth, then you will know the Truth by its fruit.

Transitory tradition/culture and transitory technology/science also stand along the corridor of Life, offering their services for the advancement or hindrance of Humanity. You shall know the Truth by its fruit.

Transitory theology and transitory philosophy lurk in the shadows along the well-lit corridors of Life, beckoning to humanity, offering or selling their services to those who glance their way and make eye contact. You know the Truth by its fruit.

Beware of the voices along the corridor of Life, which beckon you away from the Eternal Truth. Do the voices along the corridor agree with your scripture, your constitution, your ethics or your conscience?

That part of our Creator's Spirit which each of us apparently inherited will, as certainly as it dwells in each human, guide us to distinguish between the Eternal Truth and the other voices along the corridor of Life.

Watch how the obvious power of I AM drive out the pretenders to the throne as the Approval Junkies and Control Freaks stumble over each other and fall into the abyss of lost causes and failed experiments.

You have been warned and will be judged by I AM.

Recommendation # 1

THE SEVEN PRINCIPLES OF FREEDOM

A. Humans should not kill or intentionally injure anyone except in defense of Life, Freedom or Justice. Humans should not kill or intentionally injure anything except for food, shelter, hygiene or health. Cannibalism, abortion, infanticide, suicide, slavery, torture, rape, oppression, sexual abuse and all abuses of children, the disabled and elderly are acts that Humans should avoid and prevent.

B. The resources within Creation belong to the PEOPLE and cannot be owned by any individual or group and everyone 17 years and older should be allotted one half acre of land on which to live freely without any interference from society other than society's reasonable obligation to protect others from being harm.

C. Females and males are to be treated equally in accordance to ability except during pregnancy through weaning, when females are naturally to be treated with exceptional consideration.

D. The right to privacy must be observed and all religious, sexual, dietary, habitual, cultural and traditional acts which are voluntarily chosen by adults and do not harm children or anyone else are to be judged only by the natural consequences and merciful judgment of I AM.

E. All creativity, research, exploration and development should be directed toward life enhancement and must never disrespect the dignity of each individual's right to Life, Freedom and Opportunity.

F. All education, ideas, creativity and expressions should be uncensored and unrestricted except when parental discretion is applied in the home or when such freedoms are abused by racists, sexists, politicians or religions with the intent of causing hate, discrimination, intimidation or harm to the physical well-being or property of others.

G. Freedom to protect and manage the environment and to enjoy all the natural beauty and experiences of life is a precious Gift from I AM.

Poem # 3

FREE AS THE WIND

Gazed out the windows and saw; gazed out the windows and listened.

Gazed out the windows and wondered; gazed out the windows and Wished.

Gazed out the windows and dreamt; gazed out the windows and Bargained.

Gazed out the windows and remembered; gazed out the windows and Promised.

Gazed out the windows and thought; gazed out the windows and hoped.

In the middle of a jazzy, bluesy, gospel song
The wind spoke to me in a mellow tone.
It told me of the many lands it had cooled.
It told me of the ships it had guided to success.
It told me of how it had swept down and about on a hot afternoon
Leaving sweat-drenched lovers feeling refreshed, renewed and grateful.
It told me of the thrill of being on the battlefield,
In the slums and in the concentration and refugee camps.
It told me of its lonely, howling twirl through the empty space
Of nuclear infested cities, forests, deserts and seas.
It told me in a reflective tone
About the rise and fall of prehistoric, ancient and current, final Rome.

Then the melody changed to revolutionary hiphop-powwow-reggae
As the wind danced across the Open Sky.

I smiled to myself and opened the windows wide.

Opened the door and stepped into the Open Sky
With other children by my side;

Submitting to the will of I AM,
Like the wind, as our natural guide.

Poem # 4

THE WASHING OF FEET

Like many giant, aquatic Trojan horses of the sea Slaveships appeared from the West, North, South and East. The European, Semite, Occidental, Oriental and African traders; Traitors, reprobate queens, kings, colonists, gold-hungry knaves; Slaves imagining themselves to be masters stole, sold, bought Bloodied, branded and bruised the heel of Sages Camouflaged as Slaves.

Sages with the blessings of Ishmael, Joseph, Yahya and Isa to bear; Sages wearing the birthmark of Abraham's crown of nappy hair. Sages masquerading as Slaves walked across the stormy sea; Journeyed toward a time waiting to Be. Female and male, adult and child Sages lay and wait for the signal to arrive from Quran 3:52, 6:89 and 47:38.

With invisible, visible and invincible weapons Sages lay and wait. With weapons of freedom, compassion, justice, truth, reason and faith Sages patiently prepare themselves once inside the gate. Polishing their weapons and their strategy the Sages patiently wait. Mates, indigenous tribes, allies, friends and strangers of goodwill Unite with the Sages and watch the prophecy fulfill.

Descendants of the Sages, Natives, Immigrants and Refugees Unite to destroy racism, greed, injustice and inhumanity.
Impregnated, aquatic Trojan horses of the sea
Imported Sages disguised as Slaves to teach all the meaning of free.
Washing the feet of humanity, the Kindred of Christ is reborn;
Submitting to the will of I AM, the Most Merciful, Most Gracious One.

Letter # 13

27 Tree 6B2004 (Dec 1997)

Seven questions for dialogue on race

I am pleased to hear the president call for a conversation about race relations. As the great grandson of the Africans, Europeans and Natchez-Cherokee I offer seven questions for possible discussion.

- Racism and Religion: What is the religious basis for racism and are religious leaders of all nations willing to allow the children of racists to decide whether Jesus, Mohammed, Moses, Buddha or Sitting Bull is a racist or an anti-racist?
- Racism and Genetics: Are geneticists willing to debate the relationship between genes and racism and explain the possibility that Adam or Eve had nappy hair and dark skin; or is the greatest probability within the known realm of genetics (assuming we are all children of Adam and Eve) that Adam and Eve were a mixed-race couple?
- Racism and Love: Are humans of all colors willing to sit down and candidly discuss their attitudes and beliefs concerning mixed-race love?
- Racism and Nationalism: Will the media, corporations, judicial systems, legislatures and academia find the courage to probe this nation's history and expose the racist ideals and practices of its founders and the racist foundation upon which it was established?
- Racism and Psychology: Can the psychological associations explain the low self-esteem, the apparent subconscious feeling of inadequacy, the covert and overt sexual struggle or the deep self-hate that characterizes racists of all genders and colors?
- Racism and Realism: Can historians help the people look at history and determine the pros and cons of racism, and whether racism is conducive to the betterment or detriment of the human race?
- Racism and Consequences: As the Cold War dissipates and the nation finds itself chin-deep in the baptismal fires of the Soul War, can sociologists and politicians convey to the public the logical

consequences of religious intolerance and racism within a multi-racial and multi-religious society?

I urge all citizens to speak out today and prepare for tomorrow as we try to guide our children within the will of I AM (Exodus 3:14).

Biloxi, Mississippi

Letter # 14

12 Lion 6B2005 (Aug 1998)

Humans have twisted the Creator's message

In response to the July 25 letter concerning religions that condone slavery:

I support Mr. and The Sun Herald editorial staff for the courage to promote freedom of expression and the search for the truth.

However, I am of the opinion that while most religions condone not only slavery but racism, sexism, bigotry, materialism and idolatry, I believe the true message from the Creator did not and could not have condoned such evil displays of vanity, greed and injustice.

The contemporary renditions of the books of most religions condone injustice; however, I urge everyone to consider the parable of wheat and tares (Matthew 13:1-52). Some humans have apparently tampered with their scriptures in order to legitimize and promote their racism, sexism, materialism, bigotry and false religion (Matthew 7:15-29).

I believe our Creator sends messages (scripture, nature, dreams, etc.) to guide, comfort and remind us about truth and love and the positive harmony (blessings) which flow from truth and love. I believe our Creator also sends messages to warn us about the negative disharmony (curses) which flows from falsehood and hate.

Although the scriptures of most religions have apparently been amended to fit the vanity of some humans, I believe the spirit of truth which forever connects us to our Creator allows the sincere disciples of truth and love to distinguish between truth and falsehood or love and hate. Whether a human decides to hear the call of the spirit of truth depends on the motives and attentiveness of the individual.

I urge each individual to peer into the light which she or he has chosen for guidance and prepare the children for the day ahead. May the spirit of truth guide us away from the curses and toward the blessings of *I AM* (Exodus 3:14-15).

Biloxi, Mississippi

Letter # 15

Judgment will come to each of us in time

I respond to a Jan. 2 letter about witchcraft and Christianity which your paper carelessly titled "Man's weapons cannot defeat evil influences." I appreciate The Sun Herald's efforts to allow freedom of expression, and I hope the editorial staff and area clergy and readers will not be offended by these questions, which are intended to show we must be careful how we judge others because we too may one day be judged.

- If Jesus says he is not God (John 20:17, 14:28) and you say Jesus is God (John 7:16-24), does that mean you are a disciple of the anti-Christ?
- If Jesus is God then does that mean Satan tempted God in the wilderness? (Matthew 4:12).
- Who does Jesus say he is (John 10:34-36) and how is his relationship with God an example of how our relationship with God ought to be? (John 10:37-42, Luke 3:38).
- Did Jesus pray to himself or to God (John 12:28; Matthew 6:7-13) in the Garden of Gethsemane? (Matthew 26:39).
- If Jesus is God, then did God die for three days and nights and the world kept functioning? (Exodus 20:1-7).
- Would you recognize and follow the anointed messenger of God if God sent her or him into the world with dark skin, nappy hair or slanted eyes? (Revelation 1:13-15).

I hope those who follow Jesus' example will agree that the right to privacy must be respected and any religious, sexual, dietary, habitual, cultural, traditional or governmental acts that are voluntarily undertaken by adults and do not harm others are to be judged only by the natural consequences and merciful judgment of I AM (Exodus 3:14-15).

As a Miracle Muslim disciple of Christ (Holy Quran 3:52; John 18:37), I invite each individual to use weapons of love, freedom, reason and truth as we try to the best of our human ability to submit to the will of I AM (Creator, God, Great Spirit, Love, Allah, Yhwh, Jah, Truth, Tao, the Indivisible, Infinite yet obvious source of all that is good and just, I AM).

Biloxi, Mississippi

Letter # 16

Future depends upon choosing the right road

The nation stands at a crossroads. Hopefully the people will choose the straight road called Simple Compassion which is cleared by life and love, maintained by truth and reason, guarded by faith and freedom and leads to a quiet, neat little village known as Spiritual Peace.

However the people may choose one of three other roads: Irrational Racism, Insatiable Materialism and Insensitive Complacency. All lead to the next battles of the Soul War.

The road called Irrational Racism, which is cleared by an inferiority complex and parental guidance, maintained by fear and ignorance and guarded by cowardice and hatred, beckons to each soul, whether the individual's skin is black, white or brown.

Insatiable Materialism, which is cleared by covetousness and an inferiority complex, maintained by exploitation and violence and guarded by greed and consumerism, flashes its neon sign in an attempt to lure anyone willing to buy or sell a bit of his or her or another's soul.

Insensitive Complacency, which is cleared by selfishness, maintained by social distractions and irresponsibility and guarded by the beast with three heads (excessive government, excessive science, excessive religion) entices those who are willing to ignore, adulterate or abandon their natural relationship with the creation and the Creator (Exodus 3:14-15).

I invite people to be aware of the alternatives. I also warn people to beware of those who want to manipulate the indifference, intolerance, greed and hatred that dwell in the souls of many.

In order to contain the approaching chaos, which is the natural consequence for indulging in racism, materialism or complacency, some leaders will seek to bridle the discontent of the people by creating a common enemy based on race, ideology or religion.

I remain optimistic that the majority of the people want to live in harmony with each other and God.

Biloxi, Mississippi

Letter # 17

Confederacy defenders will one day be judged

Mississippi's unrepentant attitude concerning the Confederacy will someday be judged by the natural consequences and just judgment of I AM (Exodus 3:14). Until then I offer the following questions to those who glorify and perpetuate the Confederacy, its banner and all its represents.

Does the Confederacy represent freedom, love, hope, spiritual superiority, justice, truth or Christ?

Does the Confederacy represent slavery, hatred, fear, a thinly-veiled inferiority complex, injustice, falsehood or anti-Christ?

Does the Confederacy represent a state's fight to free humans from bondage or a state's fight to maintain an evil crime against humanity?

How would European-American parents explain to their children why the elementary school is named in honor of Adolf Hitler, Josef Stalin or a black leader who presided over and endorsed the oppression, murder, rape and enslavement of their great-grandmother or great-grandfather?

Can the state attorney general explain why the Biloxi police arrested me at Jeff Davis' house on Confederate Memorial Day weekend just because I walked around Beauvoir with a large chain and yoke around my neck?

Would Christ encourage children to celebrate a heritage of slavery, oppression, cruelty, racism and hate?

If your parent, child, relative or friend, whether black, white or brown, espoused hatred toward others how would you react?

I invite all citizens to stop ignoring the intensifying heat, encroaching smoke and distinct roaring of the baptismal fires of the Soul War. Make an effort to relieve suffering and abolish injustice. Prepare for the beginning by embracing the love, freedom, reason and truth offered by I AM.

Roxie, Mississippi

Letter # **18**

Rather than justify evil, why not rectify it?

In response to a reader's reply to my letter, "Confederacy defenders will one day be judged": I have no reason to feel anger toward defenders of the Confederacy. Actually I feel pity for any state, organization or individual who continues to dress up, play with, impersonate or salute the corpse of the Confederacy. After all, history has already judged and condemned the spirit of the Confederacy. However, since I agree with the respondent that history must not be forgotten or revised, I will respectfully answer his questions.

President Lincoln's response to the secession of the Confederate states was dictated by his desire to preserve the United States, and the Emancipation Proclamation was directed toward slaves living in states that were "in rebellion" against the U.S.

Self-respecting descendants of the unique slaves realize it was not Ol' Abe, Old Glory, the Proclamation or the 13th Amendment that brought our ancestors out of slavery. Deliverance came because of their spiritual and physical fitness for survival and their submission to the love, will and divine plan of I AM (Exodus 3:14).

Defenders of the Confederacy emphasize that the Civil War was about states' rights. Was the Confederacy about a state's right to free fellow human beings from slavery or was it about a state's right to maintain an evil system of slavery, racism and self-delusion?

Evil, whether in the past, present or future, is still evil. Why would anyone try to justify evil instead of repenting and rectifying?

Many Mississippians, white, black and brown, have repented and are working together to rectify the negative past by building a positive future. All unrepentant attitudes, whether displayed by white, brown, or black racists, materialists or pseudo-religionists, will be judged by the just judgment of I AM.

Roxie, Mississippi

Letter # 19

Holy Quran teaches tolerance, truth, reason

The natural timepiece which our Creator has blessed us with began a new cycle recently, heralding a month of fasting for Muslims. As the moon, moving like the second hand on our galactic clock, began its new cycle, Believers who embrace the Holy Quran as a divine message of love, truth, warning and clarification began a month of fasting, self-examination and quiet celebration.

Most of the one billion or more Muslims observe the month of Ramadan the ninth month of the Arabian calendar) by fasting to learn self-discipline and to celebrate the miraculous arrival of the Holy Quran as a merciful gift to Humanity from the grace and love of the Creator (Quran 2:183-186).

Having chosen to be submitters to the will of the Creator, Muslims realize Believers must first have some idea what the will of the Creator is. Muslims accept the message of the Holy Quran as a light for all humans who seek spiritual enhancement and social justice (Quran 81:1-29).

"Say you: We believe in God and the revelation given to us and to Abraham, Ishmael, Isaac, Jacob and the tribes and that given to Moses and Jesus and that given to all prophets from their Lord; we make no difference between one and another of the messengers, and we bow only to God in submission... '(Quran 2:136):

Such words of faith and unity, which are found in the Holy Quran, continue to guide many toward the fulfillment of humanity's potential for building a society that is in harmony with the will of the Creator.

"Let there be no compulsion in religion: truth stands out clear from error, whoever rejects evil and believes in God has grasped the firm hand-hold that never breaks, and it is God only who knoweth all things." (Quran 2:256-286).

These words testify to the tolerance, truth and reason found in the Holy Quran, although there are those who mistakenly attempt to add intolerant traditions and unreasonable sayings (Quran 69:44) to the divine revelation. Despite the mischief, misrepresentations, sexism, racism, and elitism displayed by selfish or misguided elements, the Holy Quran will continue to offer merciful warning sand true guidance to all jinn (extraterrestrials? Quran 72:1-28) and humans who seek to submit to the will of the Creator in the most natural and simple way.

The Holy Quran's expanding role in the future development of world events will hopefully be met with tolerance and understanding so as to dissolve misconceptions and promote the common interests of all who desire freedom, truth, love, compassion, social justice and spiritual enhancement. The spiritually enhancing wisdom and the proclamation of freedom, love, truth, reason and faith that is the eternal essence of the beautiful message of the Holy Quran (22:73-78) shall always supersede any transient traditional, doctrinal or political laws that promote sexism, racism, hate, falsehood, greed, intolerance and injustice. As Muslims (Quran 3:52), Matthew 12:50) observe Ramadan and celebrate the revelation of the Holy Quran, I invite everyone to prepare for the days ahead by trying to live your life in accordance to the light that you have chosen for spiritual guidance, while being tolerant toward others as others are tolerant toward you.

As we unite in pursuit of spiritual peace and social justice, hopefully the nations of the world and each individual will focus on the positive, life-enhancing beliefs and efforts that humans share in common. May all genuine efforts for peace and goodwill guide us into the harmony that is offered to those who seek to submit to the love of I AM (Quran 20:14, John 12:28, Exodus 3:14).

Biloxi, Mississippi

Letter # 20

09 Fruit 6B2OO7 (Nov 2000)

Flag debate offers a time for reflection

Many Mississippians *disagree* on what the Confederate battle flag symbolizes. I call your attention to two things Mississippians *agree* on. First, Mississippians *agree* that the Confederate battle flag is a symbol of the Confederate states. Second, Mississippians *agree* that a great majority of Mississippians consider themselves to be Christians.

With that in mind I invite Mississippians to answer this quiz:

Would Christ own slaves?

Would Christ buy or sell human beings?

Would Christ fight against his own family and friends in order to uphold a state's right to base its economy on slavery?

Would Christ fight against his own family and friends in order to uphold a state's right to practice racial supremacy?

Would Christ teach children to celebrate a heritage that includes slavery and the doctrine of black or white supremacy?

If Mary is the mother of Christ and if Mary is a descendant of slaves then what does that imply about Christ?

If the real nature, the real character, the real spirit of the Confederacy is written in its secession ordinances (wherein the Confederates, apparently unwittingly, acknowledge their racial inferiority) and its constitution and is represented by the words and deeds of its leaders, then will Christ be a witness for or against the Confederacy on Judgment Day?

Please do not think that the inevitable removal of the Confederate battle flag from the state flag is a capitulation or favor to Mississippians of African descent.

Au contraire, perhaps this whole debate is a window of opportunity allowing Mississippians of Confederate descent to consider whether the social, economic, racial and spiritual ideals of their Confederate heritage *agree* or *disagree* with the social, economic, racial and spiritual ideals of their Christian faith.

Biloxi, Mississippi

Letter # 21

06 Soil Seed 6B2008 (Mar 2001)

Will it be a Day of Atonement or Shame?

At last, a Mississippi journalist has courageously penned the words every current Mississippian of Confederate descent should read and should have read as Mississippi approaches April 17, 2001, its Day of Atonement or its Day of Shame.

During the flag debate I have wondered why the editors, radio and TV personalities, area clergy, Sons of the Confederacy, politicians and others were hiding the words of the Constitution of the CSA and the Mississippi Secession Ordinance of 1861, words which clearly show the true nature of the Confederate heritage.

Like a child calling its friends (Matthew 11:16-17), Brother Minor took a major and honorable step in his March 1 column. Only time will tell whether those who hear his voice will lament or dance.

Minor quotes Mississippi's Secession Ordinance of 1861 wherein the Confederate leaders of Mississippi very clearly proclaimed that their reason for seceding from the USA and joining the CSA was their desire to uphold and continue the evil and anti-Christian cruelties of slavery.

Hopefully, others will make an effort to share the words of the leaders of the Confederacy with the current defenders of the Confederate heritage and those who have been indifferent to what the Confederate battle flag symbolizes so Mississippians can make an informed choice as they decide on April 17 whether the beliefs and ideals of the Confederate heritage agree or disagree with the beliefs and ideals of the Christian heritage.

I invite Mississippians of Confederate descent to grab this opportunity to repent of a racist, materialistic heritage.

Biloxi, Mississippi

Letter # **22**

31 Soil Seed 6B2008 (Mar 2001)

Many imprison selves within the box of race

As a simple, country boy from the beautiful southwest Mississippi hill country, I was amazed by the lack of respect for self, others and our community that many displayed during the inferred-racially-exclusive Black Spring break. I was surprised that more parents, religious leaders and teachers of these young adults did not speak out more forcefully in reprimanding the lewdness, narcissism, racism and materialism which self-respecting humans of all hues seek to overcome.

By an almost comical yet absurd twist of reverse psychology many Americans of African descent seem to feel comfortable with the notion of separate-but-equal and seek to imitate the negative values and mores of those they claim to be oppressing them.

If the word black was left out of the title of any event, organization, business or television network, such an act certainly would not diminish its integrity if its motives and actions are consistent with the mores and values which the unique slaves entrusted to their descendants.

I invite Americans of African descent to substitute the word "white" instead of "black" whenever or wherever the word "black" is currently used in a title to infer racial exclusiveness or inclusiveness and decide whether such usage is consistent with the intent of the Civil Rights struggle. Two wrongs can never make anything right.

As the world finds itself chin-deep in the baptismal fires of the Soul War, perhaps more humans will recognize each other as sisters and brothers based on the content of an individual's character and actions rather than the color of the skin, proclamation of faith or socioeconomic status. Perhaps.

Biloxi, Mississippi

Letter # **23**

09 Fish 6B2008 (June 2001)

Unitarians incorrectly labeled 'non-Christian'

I think letter, May 12, concerning state-sponsored religion, expressed the opinion of many Americans who are comfortable and confident in their chosen faith and pity those who insist on proselytizing others.

However, please allow me to correct his definition of Unitarians as "non-Christians." Unitarians are Christians in the truest sense because they are obediently observant of the monotheism Christ taught. Unitarians reject the polytheism of a trinity, which is the cornerstone of all other Christian denominations.

The doctrine of the trinity does not appear in the Bible but originated from the Nicene Creed of 325 A.D. This creed accepted Christ as equal to and of the same substance as God, and required the worship of God the Father, God the Son, and God the Holy Spirit.

Those who embrace this definition of the trinity will hopefully understand why Muslims, Unitarians and others consider such a belief to be polytheistic and blasphemous in that it encourages people to believe Jesus is God. However the Gospel makes it clear that Jesus is not God (John 20:17). The Gospel makes it clear that Jesus worshipped God (Matthew 4:10). The Scriptures make it clear that God is one (Deuteronomy 6:4; Mark 12:29; Quran 5:72-73).

The scriptures clearly and consistently warn of the consequences of worshipping anything (materialism, etc.) or anyone (Jesus, etc.) besides God (Exodus 3:14).

Biloxi, Mississippi

Letter # **24**

28 Bird 6B2008 (July 2001)

Imagine the U.S. flag being up for a vote

As the world continues to wade deeper into the baptismal fires of the Soul War (Exodus 3:14-15), I wonder how the U.S. Supreme Court and American Constitutionalist would react if America held a referendum and 65 percent of voters decided to adopt a national flag depicting 13 stripes flowing into a canton that is decorated with a crescent moon, a Star of David, a profile of Buddha, a Latin Cross, a Maltese Cross, a Saint George's Cross, a pentagram, a Swastika cross or a Saint Andrew's Cross?

Please allow me to conclude my last letter concerning the Confederacy with the opening words of my first letter concerning the Confederacy (June 22, 1999): "Mississippi's unrepentant attitude concerning the Confederacy will someday be judged by the natural consequences and just judgment of I Am (Creator, God, Allah, Yahweh, Tao, Jah, Great Spirit, Love, Truth, the Infinite yet obvious source of all Good, Knowledge, Wisdom, Beauty and Justice, *I Am*)."

Biloxi, Mississippi

Warning # 2

JIHAD

Watch as the obvious power of I AM exposes and chastises the racists that dwell inside America and the rest of the world.

Beware of the idol whose name is racism as it silently lurks behind many disguises (black, white, brown, Asian, Arab, African, European, native, tribal) and many facades (religion, politics, economics, sexuality, philosophy, academia, nationalism, etc).

What part of your Scripture, Creed, Constitution, Culture, Conscience or Common Sense instructs you to be a racist?

What teachings of the Prophets or Prophetesses guide you to wallow in arrogance or partake in such destructive superficiality?

What application of truth or reason prompts you to hate, help, care or love based on the pigmentation or hue of your skin or someone else's skin?

Considering the fact that you had no control, choice, authority or input in deciding what ethnic gene-pool you were borne into, what sort of mentality possesses you to have such a blatant disrespect for rationality?

Do the verses from Numbers 15:13-16; Leviticus 19:33-37; Exodus 22:21-24 or Genesis 1:26-28 promote racism or destroy the whole premise of racism?

Does the Quran (2:213; 2:177; 4:74-76; 10:17-20) promote racism or destroy the very foundation of racism?

Does the Gospel according to Matthew (12:50; 23:5-12; 25:31-36) or Luke (10:25-37; 4:18-19) or John (5:39-47; 15:17-27; 20:17) promote racism or banish racism to the isle of evil intentions?

Many people have chosen to bow and worship the idol of racism and thus betray the natural will of I AM with their philosophies, theories, theology and pseudo-science; using racism to justify their fear, ignorance, arrogance, greed and/or hatred.

If racism is an idol, are you an idol worshipper?

Beware of the idol whose name is racism.

You have been warned and will be judged by I AM.

Recommendation # **2**

FAMILY STRENGTH AND HARMONY

A) Children, taught to respect and enjoy the Grace and Beauty offered by I AM, are the nucleus of the family and should be encouraged to help and contribute to the well-being of the family and community

B) The strength of the Family is based on the love and care shown by the parents and other adults in the family for the children of the family

C) Adult mating obligations, commitments and cooperation should be based on parenthood (biological, adoptive, foster or guardian), love, trust, respect, truth and common goals as each person involved respect and enjoy the Grace and Beauty offered by I AM

D) Society should provide free healthcare for children (0-17) and the disabled while providing causation-determinative healthcare for elders (71 and older), the poor and emergencies.

E) Labor laws and practices should respect the priority of parenting when implementing absence and leave policies.

F) Society should provide an opportunity for children to enjoy the experience of interacting with nature (rural or wilderness) for at least one week a year.

G) Children should be taught to respect each other and honor their parents as their parents respect them and honor I AM.

Poem # 5

The Martyrs of Mississippi

O' Mississippi, 'lest ye forget,
66.6 percent of you are hypocrites
If you point at Killen, the Klan and kind
While you unfurl, salute and worship
Their wicked sign

O' Mississippi, 'lest ye forget,
The evil idol to which Klucker
Kinda Kristians like Killen attest
Was idolized and glorified by a
Popular vote in 2001;
Showing God and children which
side most voters are on.

O' Mississippi, 'lest ye forget,
The racism of the Confederates is
What the Kluckers, Klan and kind reflect.
So let the world witness the evidence
And hypocrisy while
The desecrated St. Andrew's cross,
Winking at Justice, hangs by the
Judge's side.

O' Mississippi, 'lest ye forget,
The *spirit* of the Martyrs of
Mississippi won't let you rest
Until you repent and remove the
Confederate Hex
Which casts a shadow and stunts
The blossoming of the best.

O' Mississippi, lest ye forget,
Many of this generation and more of
the next,
Cherish your enchanted beauty,
Hospitality, potential and destiny
To be what the Martyrs of
Mississippi and God intended
Mississippi to be.

Poem # 6

THE SEVENTH TRUMPET

The seventh trumpet is sounded, echoing a verse: 'Unless you become as
A child",
As each individual, startled to reality, gather under the tent of the Open
Sky.

The seventh trumpet is sounded, shattering the silence with the words: "If
You've done it to the least of these..."
As each individual searches its soul to find what she or he actually
Believes.

The seventh trumpet is sounded, proclaiming: "You cannot peacefully
Serve two masters",
As each individual chooses the road to redemption or the road to
Disaster.

The seventh trumpet is sounded, reminding the world to "Do unto others
As you would have done unto you",
As each individual is given the choice to embrace what is false or what is
True.

The seventh trumpet is sounded as all listen with ears and hearts opened
Wide.

The seventh trumpet is sounded as each individual realizes it must decide.

The seventh trumpet is sounded, like the Book of Revelation 11:15,
As each individual checks his or her conscience to see if it is untidy or
Clean.

The seventh trumpet is sounded as it issues forth a call
That is acknowledged by some, ignored by some but heard by all.

The seventh trumpet is sounded and the walls come tumbling down
As the idols Racism, Materialism and Beastheology are smashed to the
Ground.

The seventh trumpet is sounded as the world awakens to a new day.
The seventh trumpet is sounded as Believers submit to I AM's way.

Letter # 25

Who's the interpreter of 'In God We Trust'?

I can only smile and wonder whose god is being acknowledged when the government proclaims, "In God We Trust."

If, through interpretation and acceptance of the doctrine of the trinity, the majority of Americans believe Jesus is a god, then doesn't that majority naturally interpret the words, "In God We Trust," to mean "In Jesus We Trust"?

If the Holy Quran (5:72-73) says it is blasphemy to believe in a trinity and blasphemy to believe Jesus is a god, then can most Americans understand why a few Americans may wonder whose god is being acknowledged when the government says, "In God We Trust"?

If the Holy Gospel (John 7:16; 12:28; 14:28; 20:17) says Jesus worshipped and served God and that Jesus sits at the right hand of God (Mark 16:19) then shouldn't all Americans who believe Jesus is a god wonder whose god is being acknowledged when the government says, "In God We Trust"?

Afghanistan, China, Saudi Arabia, Serbia, Nazi Germany and indeed America itself have given the world ample examples of how volatile the marriage between compulsory religion and complicit government can be.

History bears witness and modernity testifies that government endorsement of religious dogma has, more often than not, proven to be detrimental to freedom and compassion – the two greatest gifts living creatures have received from the love of I AM (Exodus 3:14).

Biloxi, Mississippi

Letter # 26

22 Buffalo 6B2008 (Sep 2001)

For those who seek the answer to 'Why?'

May God have mercy on the souls of the innocent and accept them with a tender embrace. As the world wades deeper into the baptismal fires of the Soul War, I offer this as an honest and straightforward effort to promote understanding. I do not seek to justify, excuse, convince or judge anyone. I do seek to warn and inform the seekers of truth and offer some possible answers to the question: *Why?*

- Many around the world saw the World Trade Center as the international symbol of unjust economic disparity and greedy materialism and see the Pentagon as the protector of the world's ill-gained wealth, insatiable consumerism and ungodly wastefulness.
- Many believe the U.S. government has displayed religious and racial bigotry in its handling of Middle Eastern and other conflicts.
- Many believe the U.S. government's presence in Saudi Arabia is an insult to Islam because by assuming the role of guarding the Saudi royal family, who claims to be the "Guardian of the Holy Places," the un-Islamic U.S. government is, by proxy, "guardian" of Mecca, Medina and Jerusalem.
- Many believe that by walking out of the UN Conference on Racism the U.S. government appeared to be a puppet of Zionism and missed its opportunity to repent of its historical and current complicity in the practice of hateful or greed-induced racism.
- Many believe Americans are displeasing God by refusing to repent of the sins of materialism, racism, and especially blasphemy (Matthew 12:31; Quran 4:116) by declaring that Jesus is a God, that God has a mother or that God died on a cross.
- Many believe that the U.S. government is the Great Satan (Revelation 13:4; Quran 16:84-100) whose materialism, racism, quasi-official

religion and elitist politics are the antithesis to all that Abraham, Ishmael, Hagaria (Genesis 16:10-16), Isaac, Moses, Mary, Jesus, Muhammad and others proclaimed in the name of God (Exodus 3:14-15).

Biloxi, Mississippi

Letter # 27

21 Fruit 6B2008 (Nov 2001)

Wake-up call has also come to world's Muslims

Sept. 11 will be remembered not only as a wake-up call for America and the political and economic policymakers of the world, but also as the presentation of taps for those Muslims who mistakenly embrace the Sunna-Hadith as a supplement to the Holy Quran.

The Sunna-Hadith is the collection of sayings, rumors, gossip, innuendo and traditions compiled by Arab commentators and culturalists after the death of the prophet Muhammad, and are today accepted by most Muslims as theological and social guidelines. However, closer examination of the Sunna-Hadith and its offspring, the Sharia (civil law based on interpretation of religious law), will expose the sexism, tribalism, situational ethics and cultural/religious imperialism which is being used to brainwash and enslave millions of Muslims.

The Holy Quran unequivocally instructs Muslims to respect and defend freedom when it proclaims: "Let there be no compulsion in religion. Truth stands out clear from falsehood. Whoever rejects evil and believes in God has grasped the most trustworthy handhold that never breaks, and God hears and knows all things." However, governments throughout the world disobey the Holy Quran by suppressing freedom of religion and imposing religious law (Sharia) as their civil law, thus compelling their citizens to follow a particular religious dogma.

As humanity stands at this crossroad in history, I invite all citizens to observe an apparent pattern within the monotheistic faiths.

It appears that just as the Talmud and Mishna were attached to the Holy Torah, and just as the New Testament Letters and Nicene Creed were attached to the Holy Gospel, so have the Sunna-Hadith and Sharia dimmed the brilliant light of love, mercy, freedom, compassion, truth, reason and rebirth offered in the Holy Quran.

Biloxi, Mississippi

Letter # 28

26 Fire 6B2009 (Jan 2002)

Are Muslim beliefs so different from your own?

Please allow me to respond to letter (Jan. 6, "Definition of Islam depends on freedom of the speaker") by sharing a few definitions from the Holy Quran.

The word "Islam" means "Submission" to the will of God. According to the Holy Quran (19:1-98) submission to the will of God is the original and most natural relationship between humans and the Creator. (Exodus 3:14)

The word "Muslim" means "one who submits" to the will of God. According to the Holy Quran, Adam, Eve, Abraham, Hagar, Ishmael, Isaac, Israel, Moses, Mary, John, Jesus, Muhammad and many others are Muslims (Submitters).

The seven principles of Submission (Islam) are the fundamental guidelines derived from the Holy Quran which tell Submitters (Muslims) how to submit to the will of God:

- Proclamation of Faith, which the individual believer proclaims by sincerely stating: "There is no other god except the one God." 5:70-74
- Invitation to Prayer: The believer is invited to spend a portion of the day giving thanks for the grace and mercy which flows from the love of God. 11:114
- Helping the Poor: The believer is invited to share a portion of her or his blessings to enhance social justice within the community. 9:60
- Invitation to Pilgrimage: The believer is invited to visit the Sacred House of Prayer. 2:125-129
- Invitation to Fast: The believer is invited to learn self-restraint by experiencing the sensation of denying oneself the most necessary urges in order to be prepared spiritually, mentally, and physically to deal with unnecessary urges. 2:183
- Invitation to Fight: The believer is invited to fight against injustice, poverty, oppression, suffering, ignorance and aggression with whatever he or she has in their arsenal of capabilities. 4:71-115

- Invitation to Freedom: The believer is invited to enjoy freedom of religion by peacefully living with others who may differ theologically yet share the common goals of social justice and spiritual enhancement. 2:256

Considering these definitions, how close are you to being a Muslim?

Biloxi, Mississippi

Letter # 29

True Axis of Evil: Racism, Materialism, Hypocrisy

As America and the world wade deeper into the baptismal fires of the Soul War, please allow me to respond to Editor's Notebook of March 3, "Does anyone know what's really going on here?"

Are Racism, Materialism and Hypocrisy the true "Axis of Evil" threatening the body and soul of America and the world?

If a racist can be defined as one who allows skin color to be the determinative factor in how she or he interacts with others, then is racism, with its sleeper cells of arrogance and ignorance, a threat to peace? (Matthew 12:50)

If a materialist can be defined as one who chooses to make buying, selling, accumulating or controlling material things his or her ultimate motive in life regardless of the harm inflicted on others or self, then is materialism, with its weapons of mass destruction known as greed and vanity, a threat to peace? (Proverbs 28:1-28)

If a hypocrite can be defined as one who, through interpretation of religion, ideology, creed or conscience, professes to know what is ethical or righteous yet chooses to act in an unethical or unrighteous manner, then is hypocrisy, with its propaganda machine of blasphemy and double-speak, a threat to peace? (Quran 9:11)

I remain optimistic that the alliance of truth, reason, freedom, tolerance, justice, compassion and love will be victorious over the Axis of Evil. America, its allies, its enemies and everyone who genuinely wonders what's really going on here should consider the effects that racism, materialism and hypocrisy have upon domestic and foreign policies and how those policies affect the perception and actions of domestic and foreign observers.

Perhaps after identifying the true Axis of Evil, many will understand that the so-called War on Terrorism is but one battle in the Soul War which has been declared in order to give all the opportunity to reconsider, repent, forgive, reconcile and rectify so that succeeding generations will have a brighter chance to enjoy the Soul Peace. (Exodus 3:14)

Biloxi, Mississippi

Letter # 30

07 Fish 6B2009 (June 2002)

Only the ignorant bow to the idol called Racism

Please allow me to respond to your series about the Ku Klux Klan.

Only the ignorant or arrogant dare to wage war against truth.

Only the ignorant or arrogant dare to twist a beautiful message of truth, love and freedom into an evil message of hate, slavery and falsehood.

Only the ignorant or arrogant dare to bow to the idol called Racism, whose first commandment is: Let skin color be the determinative factor in how you interact with others and forget all that nonsense about the essence of the spirit.

Only the ignorant or arrogant dare to ignore, at the beginning of the new millennium, that there is no race other than the human race. Isn't it ironic that the majority of African-Americans, Asian-Americans, European-Americans and indigenous Americans apparently agree with the Klan's interpretation of the Bible concerning so-called "race-mixing"? Apparently when it comes to racism, hypocrisy lurks in the hearts of many (Matthew 12:50).

Only the ignorant or arrogant would ignore the genetic probability and scriptural evidence that while most biblical personalities (Numbers 12:1-15), including Adam, Abraham, Noah, Moses, John the Baptizer, Mary and Jesus (Revelations 1:12-16) had brown skin and nappy hair, their mission was to make the human spirit clear regardless of skin color.

Whether they are of African, Asian, European or indigenous descent, only the ignorant or arrogant dare to use the name of God in vain in order to justify their racism, materialism and blasphemy.

Only the ignorant or arrogant will fail to understand that if all humans were blind then the absurdity of racism would be crystal clear.

Biloxi, Mississippi

Letter # 31

23 Bird 6B2009 (July 2002)

Americans are fond of wallowing in hypocrisy

Please stand and recite this pledge of allegiance: *I pledge allegiance to the principles of life, freedom and justice and to the reality upon which they stand, united forever, against oppression, hatred, racism and greed.*

The hypocrisy (or is it arrogance and ignorance?) displayed by most Americans after the 9th District Court's decision concerning the "under God" phrase in the pledge to the American flag should come as no surprise.

Whether displayed by the treatment of the indigenous tribes or by the institution of slavery, sexism, racism, political elitism or consumer complacency and corporate greed, history and modernity bear witness that Americans are fond of wallowing in the cesspool of hypocrisy. (Quran 9:11)

Sincere, patriotic Americans will agree that when the phrase "under God" was added to the pledge in 1954 America was neither "indivisible" nor did it even pretend to offer "liberty and justice for all." Such utter hypocrisy was bad enough but then, to add injury to insult, Congress decided to use the name of God in vain (Exodus 20:1-7) to promote a political and economic agenda, as if trying to disprove what Christ said (Matthew 6:24) about humans worshiping money.

Let me remind the control freaks and approval junkies who wish to force their religion upon free people that although most American laws dealing with sex, polygamy, substance use and Sunday-the-sabbath restrictions are based on religion, the U.S. Constitution is designed to prevent the formation of an American theocracy or atheocracy. As one of the free people, I am glad it is designed that way.

Taliban Afghanistan, Nazi Germany, Zionist Israel, Communist China, Trinitarian America and others are examples of the evils that arise when religion is forced or abolished by a government.

Biloxi, Mississippi

Letter # 32

15 Lion 6B2009 (Aug 2002)

"Let there be no compulsion in religion"

"Let there be no compulsion in religion: truth stands out clear from falsehood. Whoever rejects evil and believes in God has grasped the most trustworthy hand-hold that never breaks. And it is God only who hears and knows all things." (Quran 2:256)

I think this verse is an appropriate commentary on your recent series about the cultural, political, economic and religious situation Saudi Arabia is now facing.

History bears witness that a nation which compels its citizens to comply to a particular religious dogma will eventually find itself on its deathbed with greed as its nurse, injustice as its physician and hypocrisy as its priest.

However, miracles do happen and a nation may choose to enjoy a rebirth with freedom as its mother, justice as its father and compassion as its nurse. Until then we shouldn't ignore the repercussions vibrating from the actions of those who disrespect freedom, disobey justice and betray compassion.

Disregarding the verse shared above, many nations are compelling their citizens to follow a tyrannical interpretation of Islam. This interpretation ignores the freedom, justice and compassion offered in the Holy Quran and instead forces many to submit to Arabic traditions (Sunna), sayings (hadiths) and civil law based on interpretation of religious dogma (Sharia). Many have disobeyed the Holy Quran (69:44) which forbids humans from inventing sayings (liadiths/hadiths) and presenting them as divine revelation. As a result of such disobedience many well-intentioned Muslims unsuspectingly accept the gossip and hearsay of the hadiths as though they are inspired revelations.

Perhaps the sociogenetic metamorphoses occurring in the Middle East, America and other nations can be viewed as symptoms of deterioration prompting the dismissal of hypocrisy, greed and injustice or birth pains of rejuvenation heralding the arrival of freedom, compassion and justice (Exodus 3:14-15).

Biloxi, Mississippi

Letter # **33**

17 Grain 6B2009 (Oct 2002)

Most Muslims embrace the true American ideals

Arrogance creates falsehood; falsehood creates ignorance, ignorance creates misunderstanding; misunderstanding creates fear; fear creates hatred; hatred creates anger, anger creates conflict, conflict creates destruction; and we all know what destruction creates.

I can only hope that.......'s display of arrogance, falsehood, ignorance, fear and hatred toward Muslim in his Sept 28 letter is atypical of most Americans.

Contrary to the dangerous, Nazi-like war of propaganda being waged against Muslims, most Muslims actually embrace the true American ideals of freedom, justice, compassion, democracy and faith as the essential ingredients for the ideal Muslim society. Apparently many Americans, like... have not read the Holy Quran and its teaching concerning freedom, justice, compassion, community, faith, (42:10-19) and the rights and dignity of women (4:1-176)

Apparently many pseudoMuslims who have read the Holy Quran choose to disobey the basic teachings of Islam for selfish motives. However this minority in no way reflects the true nature of being a Muslim (one who chooses to submit to God).

Those of us who are dedicated to promoting the true ideals of Americanism realize that the most dangerous enemies facing America today are not foreign but the domestic sleeper cells disguised as racism, greed, arrogance, hate, ignorance, complacency, hypocrisy and the by-products of Occidental-style sexism (promiscuity, immodesty, rape, child molestation, extermination of the preborn, hedonism, chauvinism and narcissism).

Sincere believers and nonbelievers who respect and support the genuine ideals of Americanism are confident of our victory over those, foreign and domestic, who seek to destroy freedom, justice, compassion and the fellowship of Humanity.

Biloxi, Mississippi

Letter # 34

The One Superpower

The approaching Battle of Babylon appears to be inevitable as the world wades deeper into the baptismal fires of the Soul War. The souls of many are about to be baptized as events reveal to the world that indeed I AM is the only Superpower (Exodus 3:14)

If ours is but to reason why, why is America about to invade Mesopotamia?

- Is it to prevent the further socialization of Mideast oil reserves?
- Is it to protect the theology and politics of Judeo-Christian Zionism?
- Is it to protect the theology and politics of pseudo-Islamic Arabism?
- Is it to promote justice and freedom as an alternative to the injustice and oppression of monarchial rule and Shariat Law? (Quran 2:256)
- Is it to prevent the use and spread of weapons of mass destruction by non-Caucasian "rogue" nations while other "rogue" nations are considered the only ones "civilized" enough to spread and use weapons?
- Is it to divert attention from domestic issues?
- Is it to intensify an atmosphere of discord and distrust in order to promote a bogey-man domestic policy and justify the further erosion of constitutional freedom and human rights?

I believe the spiritual consequences which will evolve from this battle will transcend any religious, economic or political motives as many awaken from the sedation of complacency, ignorance and arrogance.

If blasphemy, materialism and racism can be considered the mark of the Beast, then I remain confident that the human soul will always recognize freedom, truth and love as the mark of the Benevolent. No matter what the motives of many may be in the approaching battles of the Soul War, all will inevitably realize that indeed there is only one Superpower.

Biloxi, Mississippi

Letter # 35

25 Flower 6B2010 (May 2003)

If a label reflects a nation's beliefs . . .

In response to the opinion columns on "What we choose to call ourselves...," published May 21, it depends on who "we" are or who "we" aren't.

Is America a Judeo-Christian nation? (Exodus 3:14)

- The Gospel instructs Christians to pray in secret (Matthew 6:5-15) yet most Americans support the notion of public prayers.
- The Gospel instructs Christians to turn the other cheek and love their enemies (Matthew 5:44) yet most Americans prefer the concept of warfare offered in the Quran (4:79).
- The Gospel says Christians should not be stressed out about material needs and profits (Matthew 6:19-34) yet most Americans consider such a practitioner of faith to be a bum or an under-achiever.
- The Gospel instructs Christian men concerning divorce (Matthew 19:9) yet most Americans apparently prefer to observe the concept of divorce offered in the Quran (65:1-7).
- The Gospel declares peacemakers to be a reflection of God's love (Matthew 5:9) yet current polls would suggest most Americans consider peacemakers to be a reflection of un-American activities.
- The Bible teaches that Christ worshipped God (Exodus 20:1-7), submitted to God (John 7:12-18) and sits at the right side of God (Mark 16:19), yet most Americans believe Jesus is God, that God has a mother or that God died on a cross.

Considering these observations will reveal whether America is or has ever been a Judeo-Christian nation or whether such labels are hypocritical and perhaps detrimental to the principles which "we" honor and cherish as one nation under freedom, faith, justice, hope and compassion.

Biloxi, Mississippi

Letter # 36

EXIT STRATEGY
from Iraq

In the interest of preserving life (Exodus 3:14), promoting peace (Matthew 5:9) and protecting with honor a victory (Quran 4:74-76) over evil, oppression and tyranny, we offer these seven steps as an Exit Strategy from Babylon.

1) Announce intentions to withdraw US troops by Christmas 2003 and the formation of a Truth and Reconciliation Commission of American and Iraqis to promote peace and goodwill and overcome war and ill-will.

2) Begin an information campaign to the Iraqi people emphasizing the message of freedom (2:256), unity (42:10-19) and reconciliation (9:11) offered in the Holy Quran while dispelling any suspicions of imperialism.

3) Broadcast a weekly program where Americans and Iraqis, especially the youth, can conduct an open and honest dialogue.

4) Acknowledge the budding coalition of Iraqi and foreign freedom fighters who are both anti-tyranny and anti-occupation and call for a cease-fire and cessation of infrastructure sabotage, unwarranted arrests and undignified treatment of Iraqi civilians while organizing a referendum for the Iraqi People to determine the type of government they wish to have.

5) Replace US troops with Arab UN peacekeepers while the UN and Arab League assume oversight of the reconstruction of Iraq.

6) Instead of spending 4 billion dollars a month on war, why not use these dollars to help our children, elderly, veterans and disabled while also helping to reconstruct Iraq.

7) Propose the creation of a Peace Memorial in Karbala displaying the names of all Iraqi and Iranian children who died as a result of the reign of Saddam Hussein.

We beseech US policymakers to consider this Call to Peace as they ponder the alternative, which is being stuck in Iraq like the rabbit in a Cherokee fable. In the fable an arrogant rabbit (the Bush administration) catches a duck (Baghdad) with a noose (ill-conceived strategy). As the duck takes flight, the rabbit becomes exhausted and unable to hold onto its elusive, high-flying prey and has to let go and falls into a hollow stump (Iraq) where it becomes hopelessly stuck and vulnerable to hunters; illustrating how the predator can unexpectedly become the prey.

Haram Branch, Mississippi

Warning # **3**

MANNA OR MONEY

Beware of the idol whose name is Materialism (greed, vanity, waste, superficiality), which beckons with promises of pleasure as it lures many toward its bed of pain:

What have you done during your lifetime to obtain unnecessary material things?

Assuming that sunlight, freedom, food, water, health, compassion and communication are the basic seven necessities for the human to sustain a productive lifespan, what wouldn't you do to obtain unnecessary material objects?

Whether the objects are animate or inanimate, what actions or inactions have you chosen during your life to pursue unnecessary material objects?

What part of your Conscience or Scripture have you ignored, compromised or misinterpreted in order to obtain and maintain a mate, a spouse, a companion, a title, a job, a status, a piece of land, a head of livestock, a share of stock, a car, a house, a piece of jewelry, a sum of money, a few seconds of fame, a few minutes of sex or a bit of attention?

I AM has created material things to sustain us and to offer us beauty, comfort and the opportunity to explore, enhance and enjoy all of the good in Creation for the good of all in Creation. However many selfishly disregard what is best for the good of society and wallow in vanity as they continue their covetous, insatiable pursuit of unnecessary material objects.

Materialism is an idol that some humans have fashioned with their own hands in order to satisfy their vanity, greed, loneliness and desire for acceptance, love, attention or control. Many humans have listened to the whispers of evil intentions and betray their self-respect, their faith, their body, their conscience, their ancestors, their children, their environment and their Creator in order to get money, power, sex, control, approval, property and all types of "stuff".

Enjoy and wisely utilize the good things I AM has given us and use the wealth of Creation to relieve suffering and enhance the quality of life of those who, through no fault of their own, may be lacking the basic seven necessities for life.

Watch the obvious power of I AM cause the greedy materialist to be chastised by materialism.

You have been warned and will be judged by I AM.

Recommendation # 3

LAND STEWARDSHIP

(A) I AM has created the land and no one can own what I AM has created for all humans. Share the land and resources in a just and equitable manner. After each individual over 17 years has been allotted one half acre of land such land should not be taxed or subjected to any type of land rent, except as exercised by the holder of the property.

(B) Individuals may acquire a maximum of seven acres for personal use with productive farms allowed one hundred acres maximum per individual and anything exceeding the maximum amount must be leased from the society for market value or an amount not to exceed 21 % of the annual income derived from income produced from the excess acres.

(C) Land allotted to individuals should return to the society upon the individual's death or can be bequeathed to heirs as long as heirs' personal landholdings do not exceed the maximum amount. If holdings exceed the maximum amount heirs may lease the land from society. Any improvements left by the deceased are bequeathed according to the will of the deceased or to the legal heirs or if there is no heirs or will the society may allot the land to first time landholders willing to purchase improvements at market value. If there is no heir or no first time landholder willing to purchase improvement then the improvements and land may be offered to the highest bidder, and if there are no bidders the land and the improvements will become the property of the society.

(D) All land within 100 yards of the coastline or major lakes, rivers and tributary waterways belong to the People and the right to responsible access, conservation and harvesting should be respected by the People.

Poem # 7

Most Americans have forgotten to remember

On nine-eleven or nine-one-one, America saw a new day dawn.

On nine-eleven at eight forty-five, terror, vengeance, death rained from the sky.

On nine-one-one at a quarter to nine, complacent America realized all is not fine.

On eleven September 2001, America realized a new chapter had begun.

On nine-eleven along America's East coast, horsemen of the apocalypse on jet planes rode.

On nine-one-one or nine-eleven, came a crime from hell or a judgment from heaven.

In 2001 on eleven September, strangers from the East made the West remember.

On nine-eleven during the first coffee break, man-made mountains felt a man-made quake.

Nine months into the new millennium C.E., a new America was born on live TV.

On nine-eleven 2001, the first casualties of war were humans, truth and freedom.

On eleven September 2001, many claimed to be spiritually reborn.

However, on nine-eleven 2002, materialism, racism, sexism, disunity and hypocrisy are proof that most Americans have forgotten to remember

That day of reckoning and rebirth on eleven September.

Poem # 8

Do not weep for me; I chose to die free

You may not remember me, but we met one day on live TV.

It was a beautiful morning in early September, a day my family and I shall always remember.

Kissed my children and spouse and e-mailed mom and dad. Planned to do lunch with a sibling and the best friend I ever had.

Gosh, what a beautiful morning, so blue and bright! Showered, prayed and left my sweetheart a note, "thanks for last night"

A beautiful morning, indeed, so bright and clear blue. Thought about calling in: if only I knew!

But how could I know what the new day would bring? How could any of us have imagined such an unimaginable thing?

But that was then and this is now, so let me remind you of when and how

We first met on a September morn two years ago, a beautiful September morning I'll remember forevermore.

Remember, I am the one you saw flying and dying free. I chose to soar like an eagle to my destiny.

Yes, on that fateful September day, I chose to fly upon the wings of freedom as my way to die.

So when you think of me, please, my friend, don't weep. You see, actually I am not dead: I am only at peace.

The next time you see my silhouette in the sky, smile, don't turn away, feel these words and understand why.

So cherish dearly your memory of me by letting no one usurp your God-given right to be free.

And when the takers and haters are finally swept away, I hope you'll remember me on that promised day.

So let not our enemies, foreign or domestic ones, hold hostage the freedom that our ancestors Won.

And if by chance you think of me on a beautiful September morn, remember that I am but one

Who chose to die free when and if I must die.

And I thank I AM for granting me spiritual asylum here on this side of the sky!

Letter # 37

After the collision, render first aid, then clear the road

As the world wades deeper into the baptismal fires of the Soul War and come to realize that indeed I AM (Exodus 3:14) is the only Superpower, please allow me to offer this analogy of the situation in Mesopotamia.

A head-on collision has occurred on the highway of history. Intoxicated from a cocktail of arrogance, ignorance, bigotry and greed, the driver of a high-tech 18-wheeler in the westbound lane has swerved into the eastbound lane, leaving a trail of death, destruction and distress.. Having demolished the old VW van, the careening 18-wheeler has overturned and the driver and his passengers are trapped inside as gas fumes evoke an ominous warning.

At this point in the scenario I think most would agree that regardless of who's at fault the reasonable and compassionate, thing to do is to simply help (John 13:12). Observing the consequences of two civilizations colliding, the natural reaction should be to render first-aid, rescue the entrapped and clear the road.

East meeting West in such a traumatic and devastating manner will undoubtedly leave a stain upon the highway of history for years to come, but as an optimist I see the highway of history continuing on the horizon and rising into the open sky.

Like a blind woman and a deaf man trying to waltz or electric slide to an unfamiliar tune, the recovery, rescue, reconstruction and reconciliation (Quran 9:11) after this collision will require patience, cooperation, determination and a bit of a miracle.

Whether the dance leads to romance and matrimony or bruised toes and a family feud will depend on the ability of those involved to feel the rhythm of freedom, faith, justice and compassion.

Biloxi, Mississippi

Letter # 38

Many point fingers; few sincerely seek solutions

"Never should a Believer kill a Believer," and, "if someone kills a Believer intentionally, the punishment is hell, to bide there forever and the wrath and curse of God is on such a person...." (Quran 4:92) "...Do not kill yourself, for verily God has been to you most merciful." (Quran 4:29)

The preceding verses will hopefully shed a little light on ....'s recent columns (May 19 and May 22) about the disrespect for the sacredness of the Holy Quran as well as the disrespect for the sacredness of the human being.

I think most unbigoted humans realize that whether a conflict pits Christians against Christians, Jews against Jews, Buddhists against Buddhists, atheists against atheists, Americans against Americans, or Europeans against Europeans, when we look beyond the facade of the labels we see good humans or evil humans and we "know them by their fruits." (Matthew 7:15-29)

I think we should appreciate journalists like Mr. whose sincerity and genuine pursuit of solutions to problems in the Middle East is a rarity in today's media.

From where I sit, it appears most of the media, military, politicians, capitalists, preachers, academia and citizenry of the East and West remain either hypocritical, indifferent or instigative as the world wades deeper into the intensifying baptismal fires of the Soul War.

Roxie, Mississippi

Letter # 39

01 Bird 6B2012 (July 2005)

Muslims and Christians have differences, but also commonalities

As the indifferent, the instigators and the hypocrites continue to focus on the differences which divide, we in the Society of the Open Sky invite your readers to consider this straightforward list of the basic differences and best commonalities that Muslims and Christians must begin to discuss to promote understanding, tolerance and coexistence in the days to come.

Differences:

1. Muslims do not believe Jesus is God. (Quran 5:72) (John 20:17)
2. The Holy Quran (5:61-85) says the concept of the Trinity is blasphemy. (Mark 12:29)
3. Muslims do not believe Jesus died for anyone's sins (John 18:37) but believe each individual will be judged as an individual by God.
4. Muslims do not believe Jesus is the only son of God (Luke 3:38), however, miraculously, like Adam, Eve and each child, Christ is a spiritual child of God.
5. Muslims do not believe Jews crucified Jesus (Quran 4:157) but Romans were the true persecutors.
6. Muslims do not believe humans should pray to anyone or anything else besides God. (Matthew 6:6-15)
7. Muslims do not believe that God is a means to an end, but is the means and the end and the beginning.

Commonalities:

1. Muslims believe there is only one God.
2. Muslims believe God is infinite yet obvious in every facet of creation.
3. Muslims believe obedience to God, as prescribed by nature and scriptures (Torah, Gospel, Quran) is in the best interest of humans.

4. Muslims believe Christ is the Messiah promised to the Israelites. (Deuteronomy 18:15)
5. Muslims believe in the second coming of Christ.
6. Muslims believe love, freedom, justice, hope, compassion, truth and life are virtues humans should respect and share as siblings obeying the way of God.
7. Muslims believe society has the obligation and right to prevent and punish murder, rape, abuse, theft, perjury, slander and oppression while respecting rights to privacy in personal matters which will be judged by the natural consequences and just judgment of God.

Perhaps those who have the platform and desire to create a dialogue on these differences and commonalities will choose to promote peace and goodwill in the days to come. Perhaps!

Roxie, Mississippi

Letter # 40

What catalyst will promote healing, dignity and peace?

"Why is Paris burning?" the Nov. 13 Opinion page asked as an intro to column, "Defying oppression by embracing self-destruction."

Allow me to define seven possible catalysts fueling the fires in Europe.

Bigotry: Obstinate and intolerant attachment to a cause or creed (racial, religious, cultural, economic, national).

Racism: An irrational belief in and advocacy of the superiority or inferiority of a tribe, group, people or nation.

Nationalism: A world order founded on the notion that a nation has a right to determine its policies unhindered by others (even in the info age and with current technology and markets?).

Materialism: Inconsiderate, insatiable desire to acquire, or control material interests (land, resources, property, animals, "stuff" and human beings).

Apathy: Insensitive to the problems or sufferings of others; indifference.

Hypocrisy: Publicly professing to adhere to religious, political, social or ethical beliefs but acting contrary to such beliefs.

Karma: The effect of an act; consequences; the law of cause and effect; the natural order of the past and present shaping the future; inevitable retribution (possible prevented by repentance and forgiveness); inevitable reward (possibly promoted by reconciliation and faith).

Defining these possible catalysts as accelerants to the baptismal fires of the Soul War will hopefully help decision-makers to choose between the profit margin and the people's misery as they set priorities in the days to come.

National, state and local leaders seeking a renaissance should ponder whether to continue current policies concerning the poor, public housing and welfare or consider President Bush's Jackson Square offer of a modern-day Homestead Act and adequate, privately owned homes for survivors of the Katrina diaspora and others in need.

If residents of public housing, displaced renters and others in need were allotted one acre of land and a $70,000 homebuilding grant, what will be the comparable cost and will such an "ultimate catalyst" promote healing, dignity, self-reliance, opportunity, family, liberty, equality, allegiance and peace?

Roxie, Mississippi

Letter # **41**

What conditions would end the fighting in Iraq?

"... Therefore, if the invading enemy withdraw from you and stop fighting and arrange terms and guarantees of peace, God has ordained that you stop your war against them...

*...However, if the invading enemy fail to withdraw and will not give sincere terms and guarantees of peace **then** take* prisoners of war and slay the enemy wherever you find them."

The Society of the Open Sky invites policymakers to ponder these verses from the Holy Quran (4:90-91) while they consider exit, withdrawal, retreat, victory or peace strategies.

Let us imagine the US and the genuine mujahadeen utilizing these verses as the foundation for building a dialogue toward a truce, treaty or exit *strategy*. Now, let's suppose the genuine mujahadeen presented the following *terms* of truce and guarantees of peace to America's policymakers:

Guarantee no aggression (overt or covert) against sovereign nations.
Guarantee no exploitation (political or economic) of sovereign nations.
Guarantee just reparations for losses due to US. invasion.
Guarantee the formation of a Truth and Reconciliation Panel.

Publish a Statement of Mutual Respect emphasizing cultural, academic and religious freedom.

Seek a timely resolution to the situation in Canaan based on mutual respect for the right of return and coexistence at the table of Abraham.

Establish a televised forum for American and Iraqi youth to promote rapport and exchange ideas for reconciliation and bridge building.

If these terms were offered by the mujahadeen, how do you suppose US policymakers would respond?

Current US. policy in Iraq reminds many of the Cherokee fable about the arrogant rabbit that caught an elusive duck with a noose, then, due to an ill-conceived strategy, became the prey instead of the predator.

The Society of the Open Sky hopes this season of peace and goodwill heralds an opening of the windows to reconciliation (Quran 9:11) and renewal in the months to come, inshallah (God willing).

Roxie, Mississippi

Letter # **42**

1 Fire 6B2013 (Jan 2006)

AN INVITATION FROM THE SOCIETY OF THE OPEN SKY

While recognizing the fact that any book can be tampered with for many purposes or mistranslated or misused for selfish motives, those who choose to read the universal spiritual message offered in the Holy Quran may enjoy the original, universal, spiritual essence of the message by studying the Abdullah Yusuf Ali translation while:

a) Seeking guidance from our Creator to discern authenticity from forgery

b) Using the Name of (whatever one refers to as the Infinite-yet Obvious One) instead of plural or singular, gender-based pronouns such as "We", "His", "He", etc, when *such* words are used in translation to refer to our Creator

c) Reading the word "respect" or "obey" or "love" instead of the word "fear" in the appropriate places when the word "fear" is used in translation in reference to respecting or obeying our Creator

d) Reading, teaching or living the message of the Holy Quran in one's first language or the prevalent language when possible (see Quran 14:04)

e) Reading the Holy Quran (Recitation) at least once in this Order of Recitation:

1st (96; 112; 97)

2nd (68; 77; 81; 82; 84; 85; 86;89; 91; 92; 93; 95; 100; 103)

3rd (73; 74; 90; 94)

4th (72; 80; 108)

5th (76;78; 88; 70; 75; 101; 102; 104; 105; 106; 107; 79)

6th (87; 83)

7th (67; 69; 71; 109; 98; 111; 113; 114)

8th (25; 34; 35; 36)

26th (29; 45; 46)

27th (17; 44; 43; 42)

28th (41; 40; 39)

29th (47) 30th (64)

31st (8) 32nd (3)

33rd (4)

34th (5, except v3 L20-30)

35th (62) 36th (24)

9th (50; 51; 52; 53)

10th (54; 56)

11th (21) 12th (26) 13th (27)

14th (37; 38) 15th (12; 13) 16th (20)

17th (19) 18th (10; 11) 19th (22; 23)

20th (14; 15) 21st (33; 30) 22nd (6; 16)

23rd (7) 24th - (32; 31) 25th (18; 28)

37th (61; 63) 38th (48)

39th (59) 40th (65)

41st (58) 42nd (57)

43rd (66) 44th (60)

45th (9) 46th (49)

47th (2) 48th (110; 1)

49th (V3, line 20 - 30 of Sura 5)

Haram Branch, Mississippi

Letter # 43

1o Soil Seed 6B2013 (Mar 2006)

Mental, spiritual recovery are equally important

If Mississippi's "recovery approach must match the depth and breadth of the effects of Katrina," then it may be wise to consider not only the materialistic recovery from the effects of Katrina but also the mental and spiritual recovery from the effects of Katrina.

In a column published March 3, Sun Herald publisher optimistically heralds the notion that 'New Urbanists' ideas will help us rebuild cities that are stronger, better versions of home." I wonder what ideas will help renew minds and spirits that are stronger, better versions of home, hospitality, heritage and humanity?

Whether individuals see Katrina's final destination along the Middle Passage as a sign of bad weather, bad karma, bad odds, a test of faith or "natural consequences", I think most survivors of 8/29 have had quite a few conversations with that still, quiet inner voice and have discovered a lot during this period of soul-searching. Sincere seekers of peace, goodwill and renaissance should not ignore the necessity for mental and spiritual reconstruction as Mississippi ceases hiding its head in the debris. Only God knows (Exodus 3:14) what positive effects await Mississippi's state of mind and spirit should it heed the voice of reason and renaissance and remove the Confederate hex which "stunts the blossoming of the best" It is ironic to hear many bemoaning Mississippi's post-Katrina invisibility while ignoring the fact that the state flag happens to represent the so-called "invisible empire."

Unity, peace, goodwill and renaissance are but hollow, hypocritical echoes of self-delusion as long as the state is represented by a symbol of division, war, ill-will and backwardness.

Hopefully, Mississippi will use this window of reconciliation and renaissance that Katrina blew open and genuinely unite in a manner that will allow future generations to look back and admire this generation's resolve to reawaken, resurrect and recover materially, mentally and spiritually.

Roxie, Mississippi

Letter # **44**

21 Fish 6B2013 (June 2006)

Observation from the Society of the Open Sky

After viewing the remake of "The Omen" I wonder how different the world would be if those who acknowledge the relevancy of the "mark of the beast" (Revelations 13:13-18) would consider this observation.

First, let us suppose the number 666 represents the *human* ability to contemplate, select and implement *choices* based on reason, instinct and/or memory.

Then let us consider the nature of the beasts (animals – with or without horns or tails) and how certain humans may be displaying the "mark of the beast" (animal) in their daily choices.

Doesn't the beast, if left in its natural habitat, usually tend to "stick with its own kind" or herd or species? Likewise, many humans choose to bow to this bestial behavior (racism, bigotry, tribalism, separatism, sectarianism, nationalism, segregation, etc) and proudly display this most distinctive "mark of the beast".

Isn't the beast oblivious to the concept of shame, dignity, compassion, respect or consequences when it engages in sexual activity or lives its lifestyle as an insatiable predator, complacent grazer and constant consumer? Likewise, many humans choose to display this bestial trait (predatory greed or warfare, gross consumerism or waste, promiscuity, apathy, etc) and joyfully receive this particular "mark of the beast" as they compete to buy and sell.

Doesn't the beast (as far as we can ascertain) either recognizes itself as the supreme being within its realm of existence; recognizes an alpha male or female as its supreme being; recognizes nature or a human as its supreme being or recognizes nothing as its God while it constantly dreads death or discomfort? Likewise, many humans choose to worship this bestial attitude or (spiritual?) concept (idolatry, narcissism, blasphemy, fear, ignorance, etc) and faithfully embrace this not-so––obvious "mark of the beast".

The Society of the Open Sky invites everyone to look into the mirror in the days to come and choose whether or not they will display the "mark of the beast" on their head (in thoughts) or on their hand (in deeds) as humanity wades deeper into the baptismal fires of the Soul War

Emerald Mound, Natchez, Mississippi

Letter # 45

Friedman hypocritical in defining 'real democracy'

If not for the danger, destruction, death and disunity which inevitably arises from such arrogant and deceptive babel (Genesis 11:9), Thomas Friedman's July 16 column would make an objective observer pity such a display of political hypocrisy and Zionist bigotry by a heretofore respected journalist.

However, being a descendant of African Hebrews entrusted with respecting and promoting the Covenant of truth, freedom, justice, compassion, hope, love and life offered by I AM (Exodus 3:14). I feel obligated to offer these observations of Mr. Friedman's use of his pen to sketch his journalistic integrity into the proverbial corner.

Mr. Friedman questions whether "newly elected 'democratic' governments" in Canaan and surrounding areas will be "real democracies." Yet he fails to mention that Zionism's philosophy of superiority, Lebensraum, occupation, collective punishment and its desire for a democratic Jewish state by definition implies a need for population control to maintain a Jewish majority, whether through birth control, death control, ethnic cleansing or re-drawing of maps. Real democracy?

While calling for government of, for and by the people he hypocritically objects to the right to bear arms and questions why "they (Mujihadeen militias) refuse to let their governments have control of their weapons." Real democracy?

Mr. Friedman asks "why do anti-Zionist political parties get elected" in the Middle East as if he feels the will of the voters is invalid unless it submits to the will of foreign puppeteers. Real democracy?

As the world wades nose-deep into the baptismal fires of the Soul War I wonder is it a display of a genuine desire for real democracy (whatever that means) or a display of Zionist desperation when a journalist condemns the tyrannical characteristics within Arab Shariaism while ignoring the tyrannical characteristics within Ashkenazi Zionism or American Bushism.

Considering the West's disrespect for the Palestinian people's most recent exercise of democracy, many may see such double standards as the perfect example of hijacking real democracy and holding hostage genuine freedom.

Roxie, Mississippi

Letter # 46

01 Grain 6B2013 (Oct 2006)

Pope's choice of quotes inflamed rather than informed the world

Pope Benedict XVI's recent betrayal of those who have labored to promote peace and goodwill (Matthew 7:15-29) should be recognized for what it is by all people of faith.

While professing scholarly and Christian intentions to promote dialogue about religion, reason and violence, the pope, in a propaganda maneuver that would make Josef Goebbels blush with pride, quoted a self-proclaimed enemy of Islam, Manuel II Paleologos, as saying "Show me just what Muhammad brought that was new, and there you will find things evil and inhuman, such as his command to spread by the sword the faith he preached."

The pope's subtle disrespect for Islam is made obvious by his coy attempt to hide behind the words of another in order to slander the Quran and its rational teachings (chapters 8 and 9) concerning the defensive use of "the sword".

If the pope intended to explain to unaware Muslims that it is wrong to force religion on others, why didn't he simply quote Quran 2:256 which says, "let there be no compulsion in religion."

If the pope intended to chastise apostates who embrace aggressive warfare or indiscriminate violence as a tactic, why didn't he quote the Holy Quran which explicitly forbids suicide (4:29), sectarian warfare (4:92) destruction of religious places (2:114), sexism (4:19) and attacks on innocent noncombatants (4:69-79)?

If the pope intended to have an honest dialogue about faith and the sword," why didn't he discuss the Book of Joshua or the Gospel (Luke 22:35-39) wherein Christ instructs his disciples to arm themselves with swords and proclaims, "I come not to bring peace but a sword"?

Certainly a scholar of faith, which this pope claims to be, must realize at this time in history that those who submit to the anti-Quranic gossip, rumors and apostasy within the sunna-hadiths are actually betraying the mission of the Prophet (Quran 5:99).

Doesn't the pope realize the Holy Quran (69:44) forbids hadiths and that the Prophet never instructed Muslims to follow traditions that contradict the Holy Quran?

The Society of the Open Sky (Quran 3:52; John 4:24) invites all people of faith and freedom to consider these observations as we remain vigilant in determining if the ulterior motives of those in the pulpit, press, political parties, banks and corporations are conducive to the advancement of peace and goodwill as prescribed by the Torah, Gospel, Quran and other spiritual texts.

Remember, Christ warned us that we "will know them by their fruits."

Roxie, Mississippi

Letter # **47**

24 Tree 6B2013 (Dec 2006)

Consider a tried-and-true, proven remedy to conflict

Today GOG (greedy occupation governments) and MAGOG (misguided allies of GOG) find themselves stumbling, fumbling and bumbling over each other (Revelation 20:7-21; Quran 21:1-112) in Mesopotamia, Canaan and elsewhere.

While the political, economic, academic and religious leadership of the Judeo-Christian-Materialist West and the Sunni-Shia-Materialist East wades brow-deep into the baptismal fires of the Soul War and ponders the "realism" of a "graceful exit" or a disgraceful exit from Iraq, the Society of the Open Sky invites whomever it may concern to consider an old, tried-and-true, proven remedy to conflicts.

Usually when words and/or actions cause a negative relationship with self or others, rational humans who seek peace and goodwill realize genuine confession, repentance and reconciliation *may* lead to recovery, redemption and rebirth.

Aren't rational humans blessed with the capacity to recognize when their words and/or actions are causing harm to self or others?

Aren't sane humans blessed with the ability to consult with their conscience, faith, wisdom, wit, instincts, emotions, scriptures, advisers and/or constitutional law and then discern whether the natural consequences (karma) of their acts or words are the fruits of hypocrisy, greed, bigotry, blasphemy or arrogance?

If the answer to these questions is yes is it too late for leaders of the West and East and their surrogates, servants and stooges to halt their planning and construction of domestic and foreign policies on foundations of hypocrisy, greed, bigotry, blasphemy and arrogance?

Three years after offering our first exit strategy from Babylon, and nearly one year since the Sun Herald published our last prescription for peace at the table of Abraham, the Society of the Open Sky remains optimistic that humans of goodwill will consider and choose the path to reconciliation before it is too late.

Let us unite on the common principles of freedom, justice, compassion, hope, truth, love and life as we begin our journey into the recovery, redemption and rebirth offered by the only real Superpower, I AM (Creator, God, Allah, Yhwh, Tao, the Indivisible, Infinite-yet-Obvious Source of All that is Good, I AM).

Roxie, Mississippi

Letter # 48

30 Fire 6B2014 (Jan 2007)

U.S. and Iran: Check, checkmate or stalemate?

Imagine a scenario wherein two adversarial chess players (USA and Iran) threaten, cajole and insult each other for years and eventually challenge each other to an inevitable showdown. (Qur'an 105:1-5)

Imagine each player considering its own and its opponent's objectives, options, possibilities and strategies as all prepare for the preordained event.

Imagine each player wisely contemplating whether it is best to play the chess match at his or her home, at the home *of* the opponent, at the home of a near friend or close relative, or at the home of a faraway foe or distant relative.

Imagine each player, greeted by the applause of faithful fans, arriving at the agreed-on time (2003) and place (Iraq) and doing an inventory and assessment of the chess pieces:

Pawns (military forces, spies, emissaries, spies, weaponry) are readied, reviewed and placed in order.

Bishops (moral justification/moral advice) are summoned and substantiated.

Rooks (justification and availability of funding and recruitment) are accounted for and cautiously reserved.

Knights (foreign allies and foreign sympathizers) are gathered and aligned.

Queens (respect and support of the citizens) are positioned, cherished and held in the highest esteem.

Kings (commander in chief/"arbiter of the nation's fate," according to *Sun Tzu*) are confidently stabilized and stoically *situated*.

Now, imagine that just as the game is getting underway one of the players is unexpectedly forced to abide by a chess clock (timetable, benchmark, deadline during the match while the other player is not affected by any such time restraint.

Finally imagine it being several hours into the chess game and you are either of the chess players sitting at the table contemplating the strength, weakness and positioning of the remaining pieces. From where you sit at this phase of the chess game, can you rationally imagine whether a check, checkmate or stalemate is in the foreseeable future.

As the world becomes immersed in the baptismal fires of the Soul War, hopefully all participants in the current chess game will recognize the realities on the chessboard, seek the most honorable and amicable outcome and leave the table respecting each other on more familiar and friendlier terms, Hopefully!

Roxie, Mississippi

Warning # 4

IJTIHAD

Beware of the writings attributed to Barnabas. The gospel of Barnabas is a divisive and evil invention that seeks to create an irreconcilable difference between the Fellowship of Believers.

The gospel of Barnabas tries to exploit the Holy Quran and Holy Gospel by using verses 155-162 of sura 4 of the Holy Quran to infer that Jesus never died and that I AM did not raise Jesus from the dead into life.

Holy Gospel and Holy Quran make it extremely clear that Jesus was a human with all the attributes of a human, including the natural human experience of death (Quran 19:15; 16:43).

Did Jesus ever die and if indeed he was resurrected/resuscitated to life after his execution did he later die a natural death or is he now over 2000 years old and living in the same human body? Whether displayed in monotheism or polytheism, mythology is a hindrance to truth, reason and faith (Quran 13:38; 3:183-189).

Let those with understanding hear.

The Gospel (Mt 20:17-19; Mk 10:33-35; Lk 18:31-34; Jn 12:17-43) makes it extremely clear that the Europeans (Romans, Greeks, Hellenized Israelites) carried out the conspiratorial arrest, trial, sentencing and murder of the man many identify as Jesus (Joshua, Immanuel, Isa, Messiah).

However through historical and religious racism, bigotry and hatred, the Pauline polytheistic racists made if "appear" that the Jews killed Jesus, but "they" (Jews) did not kill Jesus, nor did "they" (Jews) crucify Jesus (Quran 4:157). However "they" (the Jewish religious leaders) did boast (John 11:47-57) that "they" (the Jews) killed Jesus, but history and scripture bear witness that the Romans carried out the murder of Jesus. Who does the word "they" refer to in the Holy Quran 4:155-159? If the word "they" refers to Jews and if the Quran says Jews did not kill Jesus then do these verses say that Jesus never died or was crucified at all or does it merely proclaim that Jews did not crucify or kill him?

Will you allow the pseudo-theology of the gospel of Barnabas to create an irreparable schism between the Fellowship of Believers or will Believers embrace truth, reason and faith and unite?

Please do not lose focus of the true mission of Christ which is to bring the message of truth, love and freedom to humans so as to remind humans that each of us are Spiritual Children of God and as such we may obtain peace and guidance when we obey the message and submit our personal will to the will of I AM. This is the true purpose of Christ's mission.

Jesus did not die for anyone else's sins but lived his life in order to show and teach his sisters and brothers (Matthew 12:50) how to stop sinning and how to be free of all the negative energy which sin brings into the life of sinners. Let the message of repentance, forgiveness and rebirth into the family of I AM be the Light which guide you to freedom instead of the European, Pauline mythology of blood sacrifice of the first-born as a scapegoat for the sin of the people. Such pagan mythology has no constructive purpose in the reality enjoyed by the Fellowship of Believers. We know that each individual must answer for his or her own sins by repenting or by accepting the natural consequences and just judgment of I AM.

Because of the message those who felt the most threatened by the message murdered the messenger. However, apparently they could not kill the message. Remember, the resurrection of Christ by the love of I AM forever serves as an example of the power that only comes from I AM.

Did Christ resurrect/reanimate/resuscitate himself?

Remember, the resurrection of Christ is a sign in time heralding the end of the respite which was granted to the Enemy of Truth, Reason, Love, Freedom, Life, Peace and Goodwill (Quran 7:14; 15:36-38)

Let the Fellowship of Believers always remember that God is the One Source of all miracles, wonders, great feats or messages of truth delivered by any human, whether the human is Jesus, Moses, Muhammad, Mary, Hagaria or any messenger.

Will you believe the Holy Gospel and Holy Quran or the gospel of Barnabas and the preachers, priests, rabbis and imams of irreconciliation?

You have been warned and will be judged by I AM.

Recommendation # 4

DIETARY AND CALENDAR OBSERVATION

Individuals may choose to observe the following recommendations for a healthy lifestyle: (listed in order of importance)

1) Water, Juice, breast milk and Exercise (physical and mental)
2) Fruits, vegetables, nuts and honey
3) Plant leaves, roots, berries and seeds
4) Eggs, grain, bread and cereal
5) Salt, spices, sugar and chocolate
6) Fish, poultry, fowl, wild game, sheep and cattle
7) Medicinal plants/ medicinal products and ceremonial plants

Individuals may choose to observe the following calendar adaptation: (The OPEN SKY year is 6 billion, seven years older than the Common Era year)

	Months	Days	Seasons
1st	Fire	Yellowday	Birthing
2nd	Wind	Brownday	Growing
3rd	Soil and Seed	Whiteday	Gathering
4th	Rain	Redday	Resting
5th	Flower	Blackday	
6th	Fish	Blueday	
7th	Bird	Clearday	
8th	Lion		
9th	Buffalo		
10th	Grain		
11th	Fruit		
12th	Tree		

*A day is measured from sunrise to sunrise.

*The sequence and length of the OPEN SKY seasons, days, months and years coincide with the contemporary solar sequence and length.

*The four seasons of the body are to be measured by the length of three moon cycles.

Poem # 9

Rise and shine, rise in time.

Are you sleeping, America?

My Be-Day wish for America on is 227th:
Are you sleeping, are you sleeping, America, America?
The morning bells are ringing; morning doves are singing.
Sleep no more, Snooze no more!
Are you sleeping, are you sleeping, America, America?
Patriot Act, trapped in Iraq; Zionist and Shariat suicide pact
Foreign policy-induced terrorist attacks;
WorldCom, Enron gullibility contracts;
Bigots and hypocrites leading the pack-
Have you tossing in your sleep,
Compromising the meaning of free.
Compromising the meaning of free?
Are you sleeping, are you sleeping, America, America?
Racism and abuse, consumerism and greed run amok
State and church, media and bank appear corrupt.
Enemies, foreign and domestic, it seems,
Are substituting a nightmare for the American dream.
Betray, blame, blaspheme; bling, bling, chi-ching!
Are you sleeping, are you sleeping, America, America?
The midnight bells have rang, for sure.
The midnight shadows have crossed the floor.
The alarm bells you shouldn't ignore;
The old day is no more.
Rise and shine; Rise in time!
Are you sleeping, are you sleeping, America, America?
'The new day bells are ringing.
The new day children are singing.

Fulfill your destiny.
Wise up, rise up and sincerely be
Just, compassionate and free; just, compassionate and free!
Are you sleeping, are you sleeping, America, America?

Poem # **10**

GREAT SUN

In the name of I AM, the wandering Poet of Hope,
The wandering Tiller of Dreams, the wandering Seeker of Truth
Shall return and establish the Tent of the Covenant
From the Emerald Mound and Haram Branch to the Open Sky
Before the Great Sun returns.

In the name of I AM, the ancestors awaken,
Walk the wind and share their wisdom with their ancestors and their children,
Like a wheel within a wheel within a wheel,
Turning, dancing, chanting, singing, twirling and preparing for the Day
When the Great Sun returns.

While the pimps and whores of Vanity and Greed, Supply and Demand,
In the name of their scapegoat, eat human flesh and drink human blood;
While Gog and Magog choke on terror, greed, ignorance or arrogance,
The Miracles, in the name of I AM, will multiply and build villages in the sky
Before the Great Sun returns.

Many shamans, caliphs, imams, rabbis, priests, preachers and their
congregation of tares
Will be banished from the Gathering
While many who wondered and wandered in their search for truth and
freedom
In the name of I AM, will find their way home
When the Great Sun returns.

In the name of I AM, Creation smiles, the Earth awakens and
Begins a new day in the cycle of Life, in the season of Time;
Like a wheel within a wheel within a wheel,
Turning, twirling, dancing, singing and proclaiming that today is the day
When the Great Sun returns.

Letter # **49**

Do not abandon hope that humanity can regain its sense of direction

I hope the writer and readers of a May 27 letter ("Future news story; clip now for reuse later"), will be more optimistic about the future of foreign, domestic and personal relationships after they consider this response.

"It may be that God will grant love and friendship between you and those whom you now hold as enemies. For God has power over all things and God is Oft-Forgiving, Most-Merciful." (Holy Quran 60:07)

Nations and individuals within the vast tent of the open sky will do well to consider this message of reconciliation and rejuvenation during this phase of the Soul War (Exodus 3:14) as people of goodwill prepare for the beginning of the journey into an inheritable tomorrow.

Although its current leadership has detoured America into a situation (Iraq) which resembles the mystical fable about the arrogant rabbit that caught a duck with a noose, perhaps the experience is a valuable lesson to all nations and souls about the dangers of traveling into the future under the influence of arrogance, deception, hypocrisy, greed, ignorance, bigotry, blasphemy, narcissism, racism, sexism, hatred, fear or complacency.

Hopefully the innocent lives lost or damaged on the highway of history due to the actions or inactions of souls impaired by spiritual intoxicants will be memorialized and most honored by souls who, one day at a time, refrain from indulging in the inebriating concoctions which dull inhibitions, dismiss dignity, deaden sensibilities, slur communications, incite animosity, distort reality, blur reason, recklessly endanger and destroy lives.

Will people with sober souls heed the ayat (sign) posted above as the world recovers from the disorienting effects fermented from the "Europeanization" of Judeo-Christianity, the "Arabization" of Quranic-Islam or the commercialization of enviro-naturalism?

I believe people with conscientious souls will choose to enjoy the refreshing and healing elixirs harvested from the sweet fruits of freedom, justice, compassion, truth, love, life and hope (Matthew 7:15-29) as humanity regains its sense of direction and travels into tomorrow under the influence of the mercy and grace of I AM.

Roxie, Mississippi

Letter # 50

The thinking behind 'Petraeus or Betray US'?

Being the one who coined the phrase, General Petraeus or General Betray US?" (February 2007 on WJZD radio in Biloxi), please allow me to elaborate.

The presentation of the phrase in the form of a question was intended to leave open the possibility that the patriot who "wrote the book on counter-insurgency" would offer an honest and rational assessment of the military escalation (newspeak translation: "surge") in his report on Iraq.

The question also left open the possibility that we would witness the parroting of the party line by a general who has studied Sun Tzu and understands that the time, risk and cost (in resources, reputation or lives) invested in warfare must be weighed when determining whether the victory gained or "return on success" is commensurate with the investment.

If the question is about honesty, compare the general's testimony with the national intelligence estimates, **General Jones' report, the GAO** reports, the Iraq Study Group, as well as the Bush administration's many stated objectives, and one may find an honest answer.

If the question is about rationality, compare the general's testimony with the fundamentals of the art of war (clear objective, public support, quality of leadership, respect for nature, control of terrain, swiftness of victory) or consider the general's own contradictory assessment of the military escalation as a success while simultaneously recommending a military reduction, and one may find a rational answer.

After all, if the surge is working and contributing to the achievement of U.S. objectives, wouldn't the honest and rational decision be to increase the surge in order to expedite success and accelerate the return of U.S. troops?

If the surge is working, couldn't a failure or hesitation to increase troop levels now and capitalize on the purported success of a surge be interpreted as either a battlefield blunder, a political ploy or a blatant betrayal of U.S. interests?

I hope honest and rational U.S. citizens will rise above partisan, personal or profit interests in the days to come and exercise our patriotic duty to uphold America's "core values" and defend the Constitution of the United States.

Roxie, Mississippi

Letter # 51

15 Tree 6B2014 (Dec 2007)

Hope in the season of reconciling

Is it possible that the recent National Intelligence Estimate concerning Iran's nuclear weaponry intentions could be the first step on the journey to reconciliation and peace between Iran and America?

Is it possible that any steps toward reconciliation may present an opportunity for the two nations to diligently pursue common interests in trade, human rights, Middle East diplomacy and non-aggression agreements?

Is it possible that the latest NIE will prompt conscientious citizens in America, Iran and the world to honestly question why so many within the American government, media and clergy appear to betray the interests and ideals of Americanism and instead seem to display greater allegiance to the interests and ideals of Zionism, Arabism, Crusaderism or military industrialism?

Is it possible that an objective assessment of the risks and benefits of genuine reconciliation between America and Iran will undoubtedly reveal that a failure to reconcile can only increase the risk of further animosity or unnecessary warfare which will benefit neither the people of America nor the people of Iran?

Alas, as we approach the season of reconciling (Quran 60:07; John 18:37), is it possible that the road to reconciliation between Iran and America may eventually lead to a future wherein East indeed meets West on the common ground of freedom, justice, peace and goodwill?

Roxie, Mississippi

Letter # 52

03 Flower 6B2015 (May 2008)

Will America move ahead or continue wandering?

Born mentally and spiritually enslaved by the five faces of Pharaoh (arrogance, greed, hypocrisy, bigotry, oppression) pubescent America heard and obeyed the spirit of freedom, truth, justice, reason and faith, confronted Pharaoh, fought the Civil War and marched through a "Red Sea" in search of the ideological promise land described in the words of Common Sense, the Declaration of Independence, the Preamble to the U.S. Constitution and the Gettysburg Address.

On the path to "secure the blessings of liberty" adolescent America experienced and endured the causes and consequences borne from the mentality and spirituality of its Pharaoh generation, its Exodus generation, its Golden Calf generation and its Wilderness generation.

Now America's Joshua generation––regardless of age, gender, party religion, ethnicity, status or hue––is mentally and spiritually mustering its ranks during this election year in order to inspect, weigh and measure motives, methods and mentalities before deciding whether a more mature America is ready and worthy to enter its promise land.

Having arrived at an unanticipated albeit inevitable crossroad on its journey "to form a more perfect union," will America's decision this year be a vote to continue wandering in the wilderness, worshipping the "golden calf or serving the five faces of Pharaoh?

Or will America, finding itself brow-deep in the baptismal fires of the Soul War, decide it is mentally and spiritually prepared (Exodus 3:14) to advance toward the ideological promise land described in the Gettysburg Address, the Preamble, the Declaration of Independence and Common Sense?

Roxie, Mississippi

Letter # **53**

Imagine how Americans would have reacted

As American supporters of Zionism ignore America's "true policy to steer clear of permanent (entangling) alliances with any portion of the foreign world" (George Washington, 1796), I invite those with an imagination to consider the following scenario.

Imagine a group of people seeking a secure and safe haven after suffering and surviving a genocidal holocaust in Europe.

Imagine that group of people, without any documented or DNA evidence, claiming to be genetic descendants of the Aztec, Mayan, Biloxi, Natchez or Cherokee people.

Imagine a small segment of that group, labeling themselves as "Atlantists," appealing to the U.N., Europe and China for their help in establishing an exclusionary, ethnic/religious-biased nation within their supposedly ancestral homeland.

Imagine the U.N. adopting resolutions mandating the establishment of "lebensraum" for the "Atlantists" in an area encompassing all of the USA east of the Mississippi River.

Imagine Europe and China economically politically, militarily and religiously supporting the "Atlantists" in their effort to ethnically cleanse and occupy America east of the Mississippi River.

Imagine how most Americans would react to displacement, subjugation and occupation by the practitioners and proponents of "Atlantism."

Imagine how long Americans––with memories, hopes, prayers, keepsakes, keys and deeds––would struggle for "the right to return" to their homes and implement a just and inclusive one nation solution.

If one can imagine such a scenario in America then one will probably recognize the blatant bigotry and hypocrisy being displayed by the supporters of Crusaderism (Revelation 2:9), Shariaism (Quran 2:256) and Zionism (Deuteronomy 29:19) in the "land of Canaan."

Roxie, Mississippi

Letter # **54**

24 Buffalo 6B2015 (Sep 2008)

More than progress, debate at Ole Miss signifies irony

I could only smile and shake my head in amazement and amusement as I read your Sept. 21 article, "Mississippi's road to reconciliation."

I am amazed that you would have the audacity to promote an Orwellian rendition of Mississippi's efforts at reconciliation and progress in a pseudo-journalistic attempt to suggest that the selection of Ole Miss to host the Sept. 26 presidential debate is a "recognition of progress in our state."

Historical facts reject all attempts to whitewash the truth that any progress in civil rights within Mississippi has come not by, but in spite of the efforts of the majority of Mississippians.

Historical facts adamantly proclaim that any social progress in Mississippi has come by decree from federal courts and/or the physical, mental and spiritual efforts of a few Mississippians and a few Americans submitting to the grace, guidance and will of I AM. (Exodus 3:14)

I am amused that you would display such testimonial platitudes in order to misrepresent the reality that 66.6 percent of Mississippians as recently as 2001 chose the Confederate battle flag as a "recognition of progress in our state."

May I suggest that rather than the debate at Old Miss being a "recognition of the progress in our state", the debate is actually a recognition of the irony in "our state" hosting a debate during this particular presidential election wherein one of the candidates is the epitome of all that the KKK, the CCC and the Confederate heritage despise.

May I suggest that the debate is actually a recognition of the irony in "our state" hosting a presidential debate wherein both candidates' campaign slogans of "freedom," "forward," "hope," "unity," "future," "patriotism," "the U.S. flag" and "country first" are the direct opposite of all that the Confederate heritage and the Mississippi state flag represent.

Indeed, the selection of Ole Miss to host the debate is far less a "recognition of the progress in our state" than it is a recognition of the irony in that Mississippi, having chosen the most recognizable symbol of racism, oppression and anti-Americanism to represent its true values, will actually host a debate during this particularly historical presidential election.

Roxie, Mississippi

Letter # 55

09 Fire 6B2016 (Jan 2009)

What sort of 'change' should America expect?

The slogans of "change," "change we can believe in," and "change we need" have brought American to the point where "we, the people" should now begin to anticipate and witness the "change" we expect.

Should we expect President-elect Barack Hussein Obama and the 111th Congress to change the so-called Patriot Act, domestic surveillance statutes and other unconstitutional mischief enacted during the past eight years?

Should we expect a change in those foreign policies which tarnish America's image and seem to show greater allegiance to corporatism, crusaderism, Shariaism, Zionism or military industrialism than to the ideals of genuine Americanism?

Should we expect a change from spending public funds to "bail out," "stimulate" or "rescue" irresponsible, greedy lenders and covetous borrowers or incompetent businesses and materialistic consumers?

Should we expect a change toward spending public funds to "stimulate" the economy from the bottom upward by implementing a seven-year plan to reduce welfare dependency, strengthen the middle class, reconcile with the wealthy and build the national infrastructure by allotting land to veterans and the landless (an acre per adult); lending tools/equipment to improve such homesteads; offering modest homeownership to the poor with children (1,000 square feet per family); providing causation-determinative health care to the poor and elderly and universal health care for children (0-17); reevaluating the cost of medical care and college tuition; and promoting opportunities for jobs by subsidizing businesses which produce clean energy or participate in implementing such a stimulus?

Should we expect a change in those domestic policies which misdirect or misuse public funds to criminalize, police and penalize private, personal behavior, addiction or consensual sex instead of using such funds on prevention, treatment, recovery, or public safety while emphasizing the natural consequences of personal choices?

Now that America's Joshua generation has chosen to advance toward the ideological promised land described in the "I Have A Dream" speech, the Gettysburg Address, the Preamble, the Declaration of Independence and Common Sense, should we expect a change for the best (Exodus 3:14) as America begins to emerge, step by step, from the purifying, baptismal fires of the Soul War?

Roxie, Mississippi

Letter # 56

19 Buffalo 6B2016 (Sep 2009)

Dowd's analogy may have evoked the wrong boxer

Reading a Sept. 12 article by Maureen Dowd ("Yo, Obama: Less Spocky, more Rocky"), I smiled at the coincidence of her opinion being published one day after I expressed similar observations on WJZD's radio talk show, "It is a new day."

Regarding the health care debate, I discussed the possibility that perhaps President Barack Hussein Obama had spent the summer engaged in an amazing display of classic political "rope-a-dope," feigning weakness and inaction.

Previously, I have opined that President Obama's greatest flaw or weakness in leadership seems to be a "go along to get along" personality trait.

Whether by ignoring the Zionists' acts of slaughter and destruction in Gaza and expansionism in Jerusalem and the West Bank; by supporting a stimulus plan that redistributed wealth to the wealthy; by honoring the racist, anti-American government of the Confederacy on Memorial Day; by appeasing the anti-democratic, anti-freedom governments of Arabism; by flippantly dismissing the need for refocusing/'reforming the so-called war on drugs; by embracing the anti-constitutional facets of the so-called Patriot Act and excusing the????????? illegal, inhumane tactics of torture; or by delaying his retort to the anti-truth, anti-factual, anti-Good Samaritan voices within the health care debate, President Obama has left many of his supporters wondering if he shares their vision of genuine change.

I hope the "go along to get along" perception I've had of Mr. Obama during the early rounds of his presidency will prove to be a misperception of what has actually been a clever ploy of allowing opponents to pound away until they have exhausted their efforts, then using the remaining rounds to achieve the initial objective.

127

If what President Obama has been displaying during the health care debate is indeed tactical "rope-a-dope" and not the weakness of a "go along to get along" personality trait, perhaps Ms. Dowd's observation should've been: "Go, Obama: Less Step and Fetchy, more Ali."

Biloxi, Mississippi

Letter # 57

QYQNQYQ

Peace and goodwill be with us as we prepare for the beginning of the next phase of the journey into an inheritable tomorrow.

The road upon which America has chosen to travel at this time may yet prove to be a path to a "more perfect" society, in spite of recent missteps. The events, beliefs and social or personal behaviors converging at this phase of America's existence present a situation wherein many are choosing to sincerely reflect on the worst or best options available before proceeding too hastily or haphazardly into the future.

America's invasion and occupation of SW Asia, its gradual disregard for citizens' constitutional rights and the resulting natural consequences are allowing the People of America and the world to determine whether the contemporary beliefs, behavior and agenda displayed by America are harming or healing the holistic health of humanity.

Considering the moral and material cost being spent to promote America's current agenda of economic expansionism and emotional exploitation, it is possible that loyal Americans will recognize the urgent need to change course and steer away from the head-on collision with the inevitable consequences of materialism, racism, sexism or hypocrisy. The natural consequences arising from the theology, philosophy and policies espoused by the current religious, political and economic leaders in America may provide the impetus for modern American revolutionaries to awaken, intervene and prevent further harm to the social and moral integrity of the nation.

However, it is possible that America might ignore the apparent dangers lurking within the shadows of its current domestic and foreign policies. Many within America, whether due to ignorance, complacency or arrogance, refuse to see the "writing on the wall", hear the warnings vibrating from the war drums in the distance, feel the heat radiating from the rekindling of spiritual awareness, smell the smoke signaling the season of harvest or acknowledge the bitter, unpleasant taste of the fruits of their labor.

Likewise, many within America, whether due to conscience, faith or intuition, are awakening to see the "writing on the wall", hear the call to prepare, feel the freshness of a new dawn, smell the blossoming of possibilities and taste the nourishing, sweet fruits of freedom, justice, compassion, truth, hope, love and life. If it is the will of I AM, those who choose to utilize their common senses and unite in a common cause to promote peace and goodwill may save America from a future of war and ill-will.

Today, 22 Buffalo, 6B2016 (Sep 2009), America stands poised to begin a journey into either a dismal future filled with the potential for danger and destruction or a bright future filled with the potential to heal the past and enhance the present.

Hopefully this message will relieve suffering and promote social justice and spiritual enhancement as it helps the People of the Americas and the world to remember their role as inheritors of the QYQNQYQ and achieve the most positive possibilities in the days to come; if it is the will of I AM..

Haram Branch, Mississippi

Letter # 58

08 Tree 6B2016 (Dec 2009)

Can history help America finalize the war mission?

If America reviews the history surrounding its own Civil War and Reconstruction, will such reflections help America determine why and how it should proceed in Afghanistan's civil war?

History bears witness that the zeitgeist compelled President Lincoln and America to eventually acknowledge the morphing of the Civil War's mission from the declared objectives of preserving nationalism, state's rights, capitalism, hypocrisy or bigotry into the undeclared-yet-naturally-ordained objective of promoting human rights.

Likewise, today the Spirit (Exodus 3:14) of the times is propelling President Obama and America to recognize why the U.S. is in Southwest Asia and how the U.S. can possibly utilize its personnel, resources and technology to achieve the objective of promoting human rights.

Will the key to a honorable exit from SW Asia be found by increasing the literacy rate (Quran 96:1), aiding and educating children and women, supporting uncorrupted governance and security, preventing the flow of aid and arms to the enemies of human rights (9:11) and propagating those teachings of the Holy Quran (2:256) which invites everyone to enjoy their natural, human rights?

During the past eight years the U.S. mission in SW Asia has morphed from avenging the acts of 9/11, to declaring a "crusade" on terrorists and the oilfields "that harbor them," to invading and occupying with "shock and awe," to enriching military industrialists, to being mercenaries for Iran by replacing the government of Iraq, to umpiring sectarianism between medieval and modern Muslims, to the current predicament of being stuck between Iraq and a harder place.

Is it too late for the mission to finally morph into promoting human rights and a just peace?

Biloxi, Mississippi

Letter # 59

18 Fire 6B2017 (Jan 2010)

A voice is echoing from the mountaintop

A voice is echoing from the mountaintop,
With the cadence and urgency of a Baptist preacher
Warning and gathering the straying flock.

A voice is echoing from a Memphis balcony,
Urging the world's Joshua generation to go forth
Into the Promised Land of the just, compassionate and free.

A voice is echoing from 1967 and sixty-six,
Inviting those who heed to help the poor,
Resist unjust war and stop being hypocrites.

A voice is echoing from the corridors of Oslo,
Appealing for peace between militarized ideologies
With blasphemous, materialistic, narcissistic egos.

A voice is echoing from a Selma bridge,
Declaring the ballot to be better than the bullet
In a democracy that isn't elitist, bought or rigged.

A voice is echoing from the Lincoln monument,
Sharing a dream of abolishing violence and racism
Whether they are of European, Asian, Indigenous or African descent.

A voice is echoing from a Birmingham church and jail,
Reminding hypocritical, complacent and misleading leaders
Of their "special place in hell."

A voice is echoing from a Montgomery bus,
Harmonizing with Sister Rosa's and others to proclaim:
Equality and human rights aren't just for us.

A voice is echoing from the spirit of a child,
Harmonizing with Brother Malcolm's and many more to say:
Thank you, Most Gracious, Almighty One, for being our Guide.

Roxie, Mississippi

Letter # **60**

10 Rain 6B2017 (Apr 2010)

Are the American people ready for 'a more perfect Union'?

Please allow me to comment on so-called "broken government" and its possible effect on America's metamorphosis toward becoming "a more perfect Union."

Considering the Supreme Court's recent ruling on political contributions and listening to the dissent and discontent many are expressing about America's current form of representative government (indirect representation aka republic/oligarchy), I wonder if a genuine government for, of and by the people (direct representation aka democracy/demobcracy) "can long endure" or endure at all?

If the people go to the polls now to empower strangers to indirectly represent them on councils, boards and legislatures that enact laws for or against the people, then why, with today's technology, shouldn't the people be able to experience the power of direct representation by enacting constitutional legislation (health care reform, declaring war or peace, levying taxes, budgeting, economic reform, Patriot Acts, justice reform, land reform, etc) for, of and by the people?

Are the people too ignorant, selfish, stupid, gullible, greedy, complacent, lazy, misinformed, emotional, racist, fascist, bigoted, intolerable, naive, illiterate or too easily manipulated to exercise their "unalienable rights" to self-determination, self-representation?

If the people currently rely on and trust the efficiency/ reliability of the current electoral process apparatus (method and technology for casting/ counting votes) in order to elect indirect representation, is this same apparatus too untrustworthy, too vulnerable to fraud/cheating, too unreliable or too slow to facilitate direct representation?

While there may be a need for limited indirect representation (committees, security secrets, non-lawmaking duties or to serve as indirect representation if technology cannot facilitate direct representation), is it too soon or too late for American democracy to morph from the 16th century rendition of a republic into a 21st century model of "a more perfect Union"?

Roxie, Mississippi

Warning # 5

THE HARVEST

Beware of the teachings found in the epistles and writings attributed to Saul Paul, which are a blasphemous, divisive and evil doctrine of anti-Christ.

It is apparent that if the Holy Gospel is the "wheat" (Matthew 13:24-30) then the writings attributed to Saul Paul are the "tares". It is in the writings of Paul that most so-called Christians find words to support their beliefs and theories about sexism, slavery, oppression, bigotry, chauvinism and the doctrine of the trinity.

The epistles of Paul are accepted by many as a divine revelation even though Paul himself says his writings are only his opinion (1 Corinthians 7:12-17 or 7:25 or 7:40).

The epistles of Paul are accepted by many as a divine revelation even though common sense and Paul's own words will reveal that those to whom Paul's letters are addressed did not consider his letters to be scripture (2 Timothy 3:15-16). Also history bears witness that the only known scripture to exist for the Jews and early followers of Jesus at that time was the Torah ("Old Testament"), being that even Christian theologians agree that the current collection of writings accepted by Christians as the "New Testament" was not canonized until two hundred years after Paul's letters were written (2 Thessalonians 2:15; 3:14-17).

While Paul's writings contain some moral and ethical principles, much of which is derived from the teachings of the Talmud and Mishna (collection of Jewish theological and philosophical teachings), it is behind this facade of social mores and religious ethics that the true anti-Christ nature of Pauline paganism hides.

Nowhere in the teachings of the Gospel does Christ preach celibacy, sexism or differentiation between the rights of men and women, except concerning divorce (Matthew 19:9-14). Paul, on the other hand, speaking with a forked tongue (Galatians 3:28 and then 1 Corinthians 7:1-12 or 11:1-14) clearly teaches an unnatural differentiation between women and men based on sexism.

Nowhere in the teachings of the Gospel does Christ discriminate against a woman's ability to deliver the message of truth. On the contrary, the first person that Christ chose to deliver a message after his resurrection was a woman (John 20:11-19). Paul, on the other hand, blatantly forbids women from teaching the truth (1 Timothy 2:11-12 or 1 Corinthians 7:34-35).

Nowhere in the teachings of the Gospel does Christ condone the evil institution of slavery. On the contrary, Christ proclaims freedom (Luke 4:18) and offers freedom (John 8:32) to all humans. Paul, on the other hand, once again speaking with a forked tongue (Galatians 3:28 or 1 Corinthians 7:23 and then Ephesians 6:5; Colossians 3:22; 1 Timothy 6:16; Titus 2:9) not only discourages freedom but also religiously condones the evils of slavery and oppression.

If Jesus says he is not God (John 7:16-17; 8:28-29; 14:28; 17:3 or 20:17) and Paul, on the other hand, implies that Jesus is God (Philippians 2:5-8; Colossians 2:9; Hebrews 1:8; or 1 Timothy 3:16) then whom will you choose to believe? Do most Christians believe Jesus is a god because of the teachings of Paul or where do so-called Christians get the notion that Jesus is a god?

If Jesus obediently acknowledges that all power and glory belong to God only (Matthew 6:13; 7:20-23; Luke 18:19; John 11:41-42 or 12:49-50) and if Jesus sought to glorify the name of God (John 12:28; 17:26) why do the Trinitarian Christians seek To give all power and glory to Jesus and seek to glorify the name of Jesus (Philippians 2:9-10) "above every name"; even the name of God?

Will you believe the words of Paul or the words of the Holy Gospel? After all, if Paul was a contemporary of Jesus then why didn't Jesus choose Paul to be one of his disciples when he chose the original twelve?

If Jesus says his purpose for coming into the world is to declare the truth (John 18:37) and teach his brothers and sisters how to be free from the prison of sin, then why do so-called Christians paganize Christianity by selfishly proclaiming Jesus to be a god as well as a scapegoat or blood-sacrifice whose only purpose was to die for their sins (2 Corinthians 5:1415 or Hebrews 7:1-27)?

Only an ignorant, selfish and, or cruel person or people embraces such a selfish, cruel and evil theology that celebrates the death of someone whom they claim to love while they continue to sin. Did Jesus die for sins of the past, sins of the present or sins of the future? If he died for the sins of the future, then are all sins forgiven forever? If he died for the sins of the past, then who must die for all the sins of the present? If he died for the sins of the present, then who must answer for the sins of the future?

Beware of the theology and opinions of Saul Paul and the preachers and priests of Paulism who masquerade as followers of Christ but are apparently, wittingly or unwittingly, followers of the anti-Christ.

You have been warned and will be judged by I AM.

Recommendation # 5

SOCIAL HARMONY

A. In order for each individual to enjoy her or his inalienable right
    as an heir in the Estate of the Creator and to enhance the natural
    rights of freedom and opportunity, a just distribution of land should
    be shared as prescribed in Recommendation #3; lending rates and
    labor/management/wage/pricing/benefit laws/statutes should be
    proportionate; a balanced budget should be adopted after a seven-
    year debt reduction taxation plan based on 1957 taxation rate and
    1977 spending rate; a post-seven-year plan flat (10%) sales tax (except
    for food, water and medicine/healthcare), flat (10%) income tax on
    earnings over $40k (all taxes used for infrastructure/environment,
    security, poverty, emergencies, research/education, healthcare as
    prescribed in Recommendation #2 and government administration);
    voluntary contributions of private citizens; a 10% use of infrastructure
    tax on institutional religion income; and the establishment of an
    Economic Branch of government should be the basis of the Open
    Sky economy.
B. The form of local, state, national, international or interplanetary
    government chosen by the People should respect and maintain
    harmony with the Seven Principles of Freedom.
C. Social and political activism should be encouraged and exercised
    freely and should reflect the Seven Principles of Freedom.
D. Voting age eligibility should be thirteen and fifty-two percent of
    voter participation should be needed to validate elections, legislation,
    referendums, initiatives, etc.
E. With a well-informed populace and as technology permits, all
    Legislative actions should be done by Direct Representation wherein
    the People represent themselves by enacting laws that are within the
    framework of the chosen Constitution and the Seven Principles of
    Freedom while selecting for the purposes of security and committees
    Citizens who may also be utilized as Indirect Representation when
    technology isn't able to facilitate Direct Representation. Officials for

the Administrative, Judicial and Economic branches of government should be elected by the votes of the People only.

F. Political contributions ($1,000 per individual maximum per candidate) are to come from individuals only and each candidate (collection of seven percent of eligible voters' signatures places an individual on a ballot) must be allowed free and equal media access.

G. There should be no lobbying of elected officials and no elected official can receive gifts, favors or anything of value from the citizens they serve.

Poem # **11**

America in the mirror on her 232nd birthday

America, when you look in the mirror
What does your reflection say?
Does your image identify you
By culture, creed, character, religion, party or race?
Do you wear your years well, America,
On this, your 232nd birthday?

America, when you look in the mirror
Are you please with yourself?
Are you happy being "America, the beautiful"
Or wish you were something else?
Are you genuinely satisfied, America,
With your life, liberty, happiness and health?

America, when you look in the mirror
What does your inner ear hear?
Does it heed the heralds of hope
Or harken to the harangues of fear?
Is the message in the mirror, America,
Camouflaged and distorted or distinct and clear?

America, when you look in the mirror
How does your soul faithfully feel?
Contemplating your reason for being,
What does the sensation reveal?
Do you bow to buy and sell, America,
Or prostrate to a higher will?

America, when you look in the mirror
What do you clairvoyantly see?

Beginning your 233rd year,
Are you grateful for the opportunity to be?

America, may I AM, the Giver of Grace continue
Being most merciful, most gracious to thee?

Poem # 12

AMERICA, WHO ART THOU?

America, America, who art thou?
From a notion to a nation under a solemn vow
To be all that faith, justice and freedom will allow,
America, in your 234th year, who are you now?

America, 233 years ago you came to be,
Preying for fortune, declaring independence and praying to be free.
From revolution, hypocrisy, genocide and slavery to the space age and civil liberty,
America, now in your 234th year, what is your true "manifest destiny"?

America, two and a third centuries have come and gone
Since you declared to the world that a new People has been born.
Anticipating the days ahead, contemplating where you've come from,
America, now in your 234th year, which path shall you proceed upon?

America, standing on faith, justice and freedom as your foundation,
Are the blueprints of the Divine being observed by this generation?
Respecting I AM (Exodus 3:14), the ancestors, posterity, Constitution and Declaration,
America, now in your 234th year, can you be "a more perfect" nation?

America, America, who art thou?
An example set for Jerusalem, Lagos, Lima, Darfur, Mecca, Kabul, Beijing, Berlin or Moscow?
A Ponzi plot or a Divine plan unveiled to show the world how?
America, America, in your 234th year, who are you now?

Letter # **61**

What does "a more perfect Union" mean?

The definition of "perfect" and its usage in the Preamble to the U.S. Constitution presents quite a linguistic conundrum when one examines U.S. history.

Is the Constitution designed to form a more perfect, a less imperfect, a less perfect or a more imperfect "Union"?

What did the composer(s) of the Preamble intend to convey?

Can one be "more perfect," less perfect, more imperfect or less imperfect? What goal is envisioned?

Was the Union (or the Constitution) perfect or imperfect in the autumn of 1787?

The U.S. Constitution's allowance for amendments is clear evidence of the founders' apparent recognition of the imperfection of the Constitution, ergo the Union. Today, the religious bigotry and the constitutional hypocrisy being displayed by a certain type of American who is fearful of the U.S.A. becoming the I.S.A. (Islamic States of America) is leading America toward either a "more perfect," more imperfect, less imperfect or less perfect, more perforated or less perforated "Union."

Now that many Americans (military, media, etc.) have been introduced or indoctrinated to Islam since 9/11, does America's reaction to 9/11 reflect a desire to see the "Union" become "more perfect," less perfect, more imperfect or less imperfect?

I invite readers to recognize the growing impact/influence of Islam in America and prepare for the beginning of the next phase of America's journey toward becoming "a more perfect" or less imperfect Union.

Almost 10 years after 9/11/01 do "we the People" appear to be more or less prepared for that journey than "we" were on 9/10/01?

Roxie, Mississippi

Letter # **62**

30 Grain 6B2017 (Oct 2010)

Does modern democracy need representative middle men?

Is it time for a constitutional amendment that will modernize the intent of Article I of the U.S. Constitution?

Once upon a time in the distant and undeveloped past when governments were either individualistic, familial, tribal, monarchial, feudal or military and governmental participation, communication and legislation travelled at the speed and range of thought, voice, feet, horseback, buckboard, buggy, talking drums or smoke signals, a group of men decided to re-label oligarchical feudalism and call it a "democratic republicanism."

Thus, indirect representation sprang forth and declared itself the new and improved brand of people power (democracy).

In the 1700s when distance and the speed and range of communication necessitated that a group of individuals would elect individuals to legislate and represent them at all levels of extra-communal government, it is understandable that indirect representation could somewhat claim to be government of, for and by the people.

However, thanks to technology, in 2010 distance and the range and speed of communication is no longer an issue when it comes to an individual being able to speak, vote, legislate and directly represent oneself at all levels of legislative government. Therefore, is indirect representation as described in Article I obsolete?

If the people trust the efficiency/reliability of the current electoral apparatus (method/technology for casting/counting votes) to elect corporate-sponsored representatives/senators, is this same apparatus too unreliable or inefficient to facilitate direct representation or people power?

While there may be a need for limited indirect representation (committees and other non-lawmaking duties or to serve if technology cannot facilitate direct representation), are most Americans too lazy, ignorant, complacent, bigoted, intolerant or misinformed to embrace modernity and enjoy direct representation (true democracy)?

After all, don't Americans know what the definition of insanity is?

Roxie, Mississippi

Letter # **63**

18 Tree 6B2017 (Dec 2010)

Imagine a Constitution ratified by 'We the Sheeple'

As the Obama administration and the 111th Congress choose to casually whistle past the deficit/debt graveyard, imagine an America, in the year 2020 or shortly thereafter or before, where the Congress, reacting to 17 percent unemployment, a $20 trillion debt, extreme deficit-reduction measures, civil unrest, non-Muslim domestic terrorism and unending involvement in several military conflicts, meets to ratify a revamping of the Constitution and in the process introduces the following Preamble:

We the Sheeple of the Corporate States, in Order to transform a near perfect Union, establish situational Justice, insure docile Tranquility, provide for the corporations' defense, promote the generals' warfare, secure the credit to buy or sell and sequester the Blessings of Liberty for ourselves and our Posterity, do ordain and establish this Constitution for the Corporate States of America. So help us, Gold.

If, like in the book "Animal Farm" and elsewhere, imagination is the first step toward possible realization, can one imagine, under the social, political and economic conditions described above, how "we the People" would react to such a Preamble and the accompanying Constitution and Bill of Rights for the Corporate States of America?

Will a veto-proof two-thirds of a future Congress react to such a Preamble as representatives of "the People" or as representatives of the "Sheeple"?

Roxie, Mississippi

Letter # **64**

17 Fire 6B2018 (Jan 2011)

Some honor him 'with their lips.'

Some honor him "with their lips," talking about him having a dream
While deep inside, now like then, they consider his vision too extreme.

Some honor him "with their lips," preaching about him on the mountaintop
While, like wolves in shepherds' clothing, they erect idols to lure the sheep into their plot.

Some honor him "with their lips," applauding his work for equality and the vote
As they seek to be "more equal than others" and market democracy like it's Diet Coke.

Some honor him "with their lips," discussing his planned march with the poor
Yet they resist the notion of allotting land to help stimulate more.

Some honor him "with their lips," celebrating the national holiday
With speeches, songs and battles of the bands... but the rest of the year have nothing to say.

Some honor him "with their lips," awarding his stance on nonviolence and peace
While they wage war, in the name of gold, to control the resources, info and psyche.

Some honor him "with their lips," showing their true colors and character
As they gather to worship or socialize, hiding behind delusional barriers.

Some honor him "with their lips," ignoring his final public phrase

That quoted a radical battle hymn, foretelling the coming of decisive days.

Many honor him with sincerity, teaching the children to do the same,
So perhaps there's still hope that his dream was not in vain.

Roxie, Mississippi

Letter # **65**

8 Soil Seed 6B2018 (Mar 2011)

What is America's role in the Israeli-Palestinian drama?

The ripple effect from the extraordinary victory of freedom and people power over arrogance and pharaoh power in Africa and the recent release of the "Palestine Papers" may force the Obama administration to reexamine America's role in the Israeli-Palestinian drama. The young revolutionaries of the Information Age, choosing the pen as a weapon, faith as a shield and reason as a tactic, may yet persuade leaders to ponder the following questions and do the reasonable and right thing.

Realistically, can anyone actually "guarantee" a "democratic Jewish state," a democratic Aryan state, a democratic Christian state, or any type of ethnic/religion-based state?

What will happen, democratically, if and when, demographically, a majority of the people in the Land of Canaan chooses a faith other than Judaism? What will happen, democratically, if and when, demographically, a majority of the people in Canaan identify themselves, genetically, as being of an ancestry other than "Jewish"?

Can any individual, group or government realistically "guarantee" that the majority of people in Canaan will always be "Jewish"?

Historically, aren't birth control, death control and ethnic cleansing the only options available to "guarantee" that a particular group will be the majority?

If the First Amendment prohibits legislation that establishes a religion, are many U.S. politicians betraying the letter and spirit of the U.S. Constitution when they seek to "guarantee" a "Jewish state"?

Considering "the facts on the ground" in Canaan, is the effort to "guarantee" a "two-state solution" an example of freedom and democracy or arrogance and hypocrisy?

According to monotheistic scriptures, Ishmael and Isaac never had a problem with each other but just happened to be caught up in the middle of a "babies' mommas drama".

I wonder how and when the drama will finally end.

Roxie, Mississippi

Letter # 66

Dancing with the devil while children and women suffer

After reading Kathleen Parker's recent article ("It's the women, stupid") about the Obama administration's desire to dance with the devil and betray the children and women of Afghanistan by appeasing the Karzai government and Taliban, I was left wondering why most Muslim women, especially in the West, are not as aggressive as Ms. Parker in speaking out and proclaiming to the men in their lives that Muslim women will no longer submit to the expectations, stereotypes, laws or dogma which deprive many Muslim women of their God-given right to be free.

Is it due to illiteracy, fear, faith, apathy or insecurity that most Muslim women fail to question the legitimacy of traditions, sayings or laws which disrespect their faith (Quran 2:256), fondle their individualism, assault their common sense, ravish their potential, abuse their love, molest their honor and rape their spiritual peace?

Is it due to wickedness, insecurity, fear, faith or Freudianism that most Muslim men continue to be complicit in the betrayal, abuse and enslavement of their daughters, mothers, sisters, aunts, nieces, cousins, mates and other women who are being victimized by fraudulent, anti-Quranic, satanic versions of sunna-hadith or sharia law?

Ignoring the empirical evidence that human history is a spiritual/mental struggle, the capitalist and socialist adherents of the Marxist theory that history is an economic/materialist struggle are desperately trying to balance their sincere pursuit of wealth and power with their hypocritical declarations of human rights, as if trying to prove they can "serve two masters." (Matthew 6:24)

The current winds of revolution are turning a new page in the age of reason and will hopefully guide many to realize that in the Soul War (Exodus 3:14) children's and women's rights are the basis and epitome of human rights and should not be compromised, delayed or betrayed.

Roxie, Mississippi

Letter # 67

3 Fish 6B2018 (June 2011)

Osama bin Laden's death could clear air

The death of the "useful" zealot Osama bin Laden could be the pivotal event which opens a new chapter in the relationship between those in America and the Middle East who genuinely seek to promote freedom and human rights.

Osama Bin Laden, much like the character Goldstein in George Orwell's "1984," served as a "useful" image for religious and racial bigots, economic and political puppeteers, the military industrial complex and the mis-informative media which exploited the persona of bin Laden by trying to make him and his followers the face of the enemy, the face of the "other" or the face of Islam.

Now that bin Laden has been removed as the mascot for the manipulative and bigoted elements in America and the Middle East, I am optimistic that the promoters of human rights can refocus on shared commonalities. While rejecting the use of indiscriminate violence and any interpretation of religion which hinders human rights, people of goodwill also reject and seek to change those domestic and foreign policies which hinder the struggle for freedom and human rights.

Whether it is the Orwellian "Patriot Act" and economic/political elitism in America, Zionist racism and occupation/apartheid in Canaan, corruption and religious/gender bigotry in Arabia, Asia, Africa and Europe or the exploitation of workers, the poor, resources and the environment throughout the world, such policies remain as a hindrance to freedom and human rights.

The demise of bin Laden, the eventual release of incriminating information confiscated from his "cave" and the gradual irrelevancy and obsolescence of Shariaism, Crusaderism, Zionism, Caliphism and Egocapitalism will perhaps enhance the opportunity for good people to cooperate more harmoniously and continue the jihad (struggle) for freedom and human rights.

Natchez / Roxie, Mississippi

Letter # **68**

A dream fulfilled... or a mirage slowly fading?

If Rev. King could visit President Obama to discuss war and poverty, would he be pleased or disappointed with the administration's current policy?

If Dr. King could speak to the occupiers of Congress, the mall, Main and Wall streets, would he make materialism, vanity, vice and "vulture capitalism" the focus of his speech?

If Rev. King could travel to Jerusalem to promote peace and pray, would he recommend a Jim Crow two-state or a democratic one-nation solution as the American way?

If Dr. King could examine America's national, racial, religious, political and economic ego and id, what would be his diagnosis and what would he prescribe or forbid?

If Rev. King could witness the current dropout, teen pregnancy, crime, sentencing, voting, poverty or tax rate, how would he react when he compared 2012 facts, figures and statistics to 1968?

If Dr. King could meet with bankers, businesses and economists, would posterity, environment, wages, prices, profits, austerity, land and opportunity be on his priority list?

If Rev. King could drive along the boulevard bearing his name, would he smile with pride or frown with shame?

If Dr. King could comment on the NDAA, the Patriot Act and other attacks on the Constitution today, would he warn America's "Joshua generation" to keep our "eyes on the prize" and don't be led astray?

If Dr/Rev. King could address the issues that America and the world are now facing, would he describe a dream being fulfilled or a mirage slowly fading?

Roxie, Mississippi

Letter # **69**

Campaign Shellgame

If, according to capitalism, minimizing the cost of labor
While maximizing the amount of profit is truly savored
Then high unemployment and underemployment work in whose favor?

"Jobs, jobs, jobs", is the manipulative mantra the politicians purr
As they and the media choose the issue they most prefer
To distract the people while their puppeteers plot and prosper.

If America has an 82 to 90 percent employment rate
Shouldn't wages, prices, profits and greed and how, to jobs, they relate
Be the real issue that most people encourage their representatives to embrace?

"Wages, prices, profits", is a mantra often long ignored.
Until the peasants storm the bastille, bank, castle, plantation or corporate doors
And a reasonable distribution of land, opportunity, justice and order is restored.

If the purpose of the con-man is to profit by gaining the people's confidence
And politicians, bankers and economist openly declare the same policy and intent
Then who bears the blame and the responsibility for the natural consequence?

Utilizing child labor, illegal immigration, outsourcing, beasts of burden,
Sharecropping, minimum wage, slavery or serfdom,
Cheap or free labor to maximize profit has always been the wizard behind the curtain.

Whether history is a reflection of humanity's spiritual struggle

Or, as Marx and Madoff's mantra suggest, materialism is the source of the toil and trouble,
Doesn't the message of Matthew 19:21-26 remain equally explicit and subtle?

So as we hear the slogans and mantras during the campaigns of 2012
And consider what the politicians, the media and their puppeteers are trying to sell
Hopefully America won't be bamboozled by the sleight-of-hand shuffling of the shells.

Natchez, Mississippi

Letter # 70

21 Flower 6B2019 (May 2012)

Separation of Bigotry & Faith

President Obama's recent comments about same-gender matrimony and equal rights have brought America to the intersection of religious bigotry boulevard, social semantics street, theological hypocrisy highway and constitutional rights road.

When certain Americans use their scripture to define marriage while discriminately disrespecting and rejecting the tradition of polygamy as practiced and prescribed in the Old Testament and Holy Quran, are they displaying symptoms of religious bigotry?

If providing a happy and healthy environment for children is the natural, unscripted, historical and divine essence of the spiritual, psychological, physiological, economic and familial commitment between consenting adults, then isn't it merely social semantics whether one uses the term marriage, civil union, common law, soul mates or parenthood to describe the commitment?

When Paulinian Americans point an accusatory finger at the institution of sharia law (civil law based on religious interpretation) in the Middle East while they seek to legislatively impose their own situational interpretation of Paul's opinions (1 Corinthians 7:12-17 / 7:40) in America, are they an example of theological hypocrisy?

Is it theological hypocrisy when some Americans "cast the first stone" while they willingly disobey and legislatively disregard their denominational translations of Jesus' teachings concerning divorce (Mt 19:3 / 19:7-9), marriage (Mt 19:4-6 / 19:10-11/ 22:29-30; Lk 17:24-30), abortion (Mt 19:13-17 / 18:1-14) fornication or adultery?

If, as an American citizen, I cherish the right to share a consensual, committed relationship with the woman or women I love, trust and respect, would I be a bigot, hypocrite, narcissist or Jim Crowist if I used my religious belief or misbelief or unbelief to deny another citizen the opportunity to enjoy the equal rights prescribed by the U.S. Constitution?

Is America a constitutional, democratic republic or a biblical, pseudo-Christian Plutheocracy and which path will we choose as we journey into the future?

Roxie & Jackson, Mississippi

Letter # 71

21 Fish 6B2019 (June 2012)

An Exorcism in the Age of Reason

Today heralds the arrival of "E-Day" as the evil spirits which have possessed the current society begin to experience the effects of a societal exorcism. Observing the events in the weeks and months to come, one will witness the reactions to and the results of this modern-day casting out of ungodly influences.

If one will consider religion, politics, economics, media, security, family and individuality to be the seven pillars of human society it appears that evil influences are gnawing, scratching, clawing and undermining the seven pillars and therefore weakening the structural integrity and health of the current society.

In order to proceed with this societal exorcism there are seven fundamental steps which must be taken to achieve the objective, which is, God willing, to cast out the evil influences and restore the structural integrity and health of human society for ourselves and future generations.

Step 1. Shine light on the evil spirits by acknowledging that there is something effecting society which is diabolically sinister, antihuman and inconsistent with hope, love and the law and order of Creation.

Step 2. Identify the evil spirits:

a) Blasphemy (inventing lies, rituals, religions, mythology and false scriptures which claim to be the "word of God" but are actually the antithesis to the truth, law and order of Creation which is the only indisputable, unalterable, infinite-yet-obvious true Word of God.)

b) Vanity (promoting narcissism, tribalism, racism, sexism, hatred, sectarianism, nationalism, elitism or monarchism)

c) Greed (exploiting, monopolizing or hoarding wealth, power, resources, land, labor, wages, profits, consumption or deprivation)

d) Deception (engaging in lies, misinformation or hypocrisy in pursuit of profit, pleasure, power or influence)

e) Criminality (causing harm to others in pursuit of profit, pleasure, power or influence)

f) Corruption (misusing or abusing the expectations and responsibility of leadership in pursuit of profit, pleasure, power or influence)

g) Ignorance (ignoring, rejecting, hiding, hindering or lacking pertinent or pragmatic facts)

Step 3. Bind the evil spirits with the rope of Truth.

Step 4. Drown the evil spirits with the water of Reason.

Step 5. Dismember the evil spirits with the sword of Justice.

Step 6. Burn the evil spirits with the fire of Freedom

Step 7. Cast out the evil spirits with the wind of Rebirth

The implementation of the seven steps of exorcism prescribed herein will restore the structural integrity and health of humanity, if it is the will of God.

As humanity proceeds farther along the path into the "Age of Reason" and emerges from the baptismal fires of the Soul War I invite you to bear witness to the reactions and results generated by the commencement of the societal exorcism which begins today.

Haram Branch, Mississippi

Letter # 72

12 Bird 6B2019 (July 2012)

Is It Just Me?

Is it just me or does anyone else see the sad irony in witnessing the Zionist today building massive walls in order to concentrate Jews within a well-fortified encampment as a final solution for securing ample lebensraum, a particular religious/racial identity and a Jim Crow pseudo-democracy?

Is it just me or does anyone else find it insulting that politicians and the media seek to make "jobs, jobs, jobs, taxes, taxes, taxes" the Orwellian mantra during election time while conveniently ignoring the fact that if the unemployment rate is ten percent then the ninety percent that is employed probably thinks prices, profits and wages, as well as the encroachment on privacy and constitutional rights, are the most important issues?

Is it just me or does anyone else hears the deafening silence since the beginning of the Arab spring emanating from those who post 9-11 vehemently and prejudicially proclaimed "they hate us because of our freedom"?

Is it just me or does anyone else wonder why anyone would publish a full page of theological quotes on Independence Day yet blatantly ignore the pro-Deity and anti-Biblical quotes from The Age of Reason which was written by the most fervent, logical and enlightened advocate for American independence, Thomas Paine?

Is it just me or does anyone else finds it suspiciously odd that if the entire Bible is true then why do Matthew and Luke, leaving seekers of the truth to ponder which is the truth (wheat) or the lie (tares), give a contradicting genealogy for Jesus extending from David to Joseph?

Is it just me or does anyone else feels such questions as these are even relevant as the Americas emerge from the baptismal fires of the Soul War and journey into the future?

Haram Branch, Mississippi

Warning # 6

HEGIRA/HIGRA

Beware of the doctrine of the "Sunna-Hadith". It is a blasphemous, divisive, evil doctrine designed to derail the mission of the Prophet and divide and scatter the Fellowship of Believers. (Holy Quran 6:89)

Turn away from the voices of gossip and the chains of tradition, which betray the Prophet and accuse Muhammad of adding to the Holy Quran. The Prophet Muhammad never added any saying to the Holy Quran (69:44 or 27:89-93).

Will you believe the words of the Holy Quran or will you believe the words of the Sunna -Hadith and Shariat - even if they contradict the Holy Quran?

Have you ever heard of a weak hadith? Have you ever heard of a weak ayat? Does the Sunna Hadith of the Sunni sect correlate with the Hadith Sunna of the Shia sect?

If not, then which one is the truth and which one is falsehood (23:90)? Doesn't the Quran teach us that Abraham is the model for all Muslims to consider? Did Abraham follow the Sunna Hadith or Sharia law?

If many Muslims believe they must add the Sunna Hadith and Sharia law to the Holy Quran, then how does such a belief reconcile with these verses from the Holy Quran:

75:13-21; 69:44; 57:25-29; 54:38-40; 50:45; 46:8-10; 43:43-45; 41:40-43; 39:22-41; 36:69-70; 33:18-21; 27:1-19; 26:192-227; 16:120-123; 13:38-40; 10:15-17; 9:101-110; 5:48-50; 3:138-148?

Perhaps it is time for those who have strayed from the universal, spiritual message offered in the Holy Quran to reconsider their path and take steps to return to the original essence of the message.

The Arabization of Islam and the assimilation displayed by those who sincerely mimic the misguided ones have aided the enemies of Islam and misled many onto the path of reactionary tribalism, materialism, sexism, complacency and spiritual bondage or onto the path to rejection of Islam.

Are those who arrogantly ignore the Holy Quran's invitation to spiritual freedom and instead choose to add or subtract from the original Message by compelling (Quran 2:256) others to submit to sunna-hadith or sharia law a reflection of truth and reason (Quran 17:81) or falsehood and foolishness?

You have been warned and will be judged by I AM.

Recommendation # 6

JUSTICE AND SECURITY

A) Within a just Judicial System: Violent crimes (murder, rape, child abuse, elderly abuse, disabled abuse, treason, assault, kidnapping, etc, or conspiracy to commit such acts) are punishable by: permanent banishment to island or other designated areas set aside for specific violent crimes with families or charity providing non-essentials and the society providing food, water and shelter or punishment issued by victim or victim's next of kin

B) Nonviolent crimes (theft, perjury, harassment, vandalism, sexism racism, discrimination., endangerment, threatening, stalking, violation of house arrest, violation of specified monitoring, etc. or conspiracy to commit such acts) are punishable by: temporary banishment to designated areas set aside for specific non-violent crimes "with families or charities providing nonessentials and the society providing food, water and shelter or punishment issued by victim or victim's next of kin based on forgiveness, compensatory service to victim or victim deciding reasonable length of banishment

C) Jails are maintained to hold those accused of violent crimes until trial and sentencing. Those accused of nonviolent crimes are subjected to ticketing, house-arrest or electronic monitoring until trial and sentencing. Each citizen has a right to legal representation.

D) Mandatory, just compensation must be awarded to those arrested, jailed or banished unjustly.

E) No laws are to be made which punish adults for engaging in personal freedoms (sexual, habitual, religious, dietary, hygienic etc) which do not harm others. The rights of the individual, natural consequences and just judgment of I AM should be respected.

F) Adults (17-47) should serve at least two years in the military or other public service in order to protect and promote the principles of Freedom, Justice and Security and Relieve / Abolish Suffering.

G) In the Conduct of War it may be best to observe the following steps to security:

1] Maintain a Sense of Vigilance and Prevention and Be Prepared.

2] Seek a relationship of Peace and Goodwill with All who seek Peace and Goodwill.

3] Seek a relationship of War and Reconciliation with Enemy who threatens you or yours.

4] Seek a relationship of War and Rehabilitation with Enemy who attacks you or yours.

5] Seek a relationship of War and Rehabilitation to protect the Innocent and Oppressed

6] Seek a relationship of War and Annihilation with Enemy who Refuses to Rehabilitate

7] Respect all contracts, treaties or agreements with those who do not threaten the opportunity to enjoy freedom, justice, truth, compassion, hope, love or life and children shouldn't be intentionally targeted or knowingly utilized as combatants or shields during warfare.

Poem # **13**

A CHILD SHALL LEAD THEM

I hear a voice in my head;
The voice of a young child apparently well-read.
The voice, the tiny voice
Tells me to write-
Describing and dictating what I must bring to the Light.
Obedient to the voice and its desire to make things right
I write what I am told before the coming of the night.

Sometimes from the lightning, thunder or the hummingbird hover
The voice gently dictates; a voice unlike any other.
Yes, the voice quietly chooses, arranges and edits the words
Which serve as wings for the Soul to soar higher than celestial birds.
The words keep coming and I obediently obey
Because now I understand how a Child shall lead the way.

A friend asked me how, when and where do the words come from.
I try to explain; from the rain, hills, forest, banjo, drum, woodwind, earth,
Sky and beyond.
But how can I explain a voice that only I hear?
How can I explain this friendship I cherish so dear?
The tiny voice wielding words like a sword tells me what to say
As we both, the child and I, joyfully submit to I AM's way.

So I write and I write as if I have no choice;
As if I've become one with the tiny, mystical
And childish voice.
And I guess in a way, somehow we are one and the same
Since we both choose to obediently bow to the sacred Name.

Together we stand, child and adult, like a lion and lamb;
Sharpening the sword and polishing the gavel;
Sowing the seed and gathering the harvest;
As servants of I AM

Poem # **14**

WHAT WILL CHRIST SAY?

What will Christ say?
When Christ returns someday
And finds those who call him Lord
Teaching innocent Children that Jesus is God?
What will Christ say?
On that dreadful and glorious day?

What will Christ say?
When Christ returns someday
And finds the lying politician, selfish consumer and greedy businessman
Abusing the children, the poor, the innocent and ignorant
By waging war, worshipping gold and raping the land?
What will Christ say?
On that dreadful and glorious day?

What will Christ say?
When Christ returns someday
And finds the few disciples who dare to experience colorblind love
Being disrespected and despised
By humans with skin of different hue but the same human blood?
What will Christ say?
On that dreadful and glorious day?

What will Christ say?
When Christ returns someday
And finds many eating from the Blasphemy Tree,
Worshipping that golden calf known as the trinity?
What **will** Christ say?
On that dreadful and glorious day?

What will Christ say?
When Christ returns someday

And finds the preachers of Paulism urging innocent children to
Comprehend
The Apostate Paul's twisted theory of "original sin"?
What will Christ say?
On that dreadful and glorious day?

What will Christ say?
When Christ returns someday
And finds the racists, bigots and their kind and clan
Wearing, twisting, bending and burning crosses,
Trying to rewrite or undo the Divine Plan?
What will Christ say?
On that dreadful and glorious day?

What will Christ say?
When Christ returns someday
And finds many preachers, priests and their followers betraying the lamb
By worshipping Jesus as their god instead of giving all glory to I AM?
What **will** Christ say?
On that dreadful and glorious day?

What will Christ say?
When Christ returns someday
And I Am, the judge of all, asks whether Christ's disciples have been true;
How will Christ answer when Christ bears witness for or against you?
What will Christ say?
On that dreadful and glorious day?

Letter # 73

Freedom of Expression; Freedom of Reaction?

Peace and Goodwill!
The events stemming from an anti-Muslim film and advertisement have opened a window of opportunity to consider the relationship between freedom of expression and freedom of reaction.

Whether the makers of the advertisement or the film intended to misinform, inform, insult or incite, the freedom of reaction leaves "all options on the table" ranging from enjoying it, ignoring it or answering in-kind to responding with censorship, anger, nonviolence or violence.

Afterall, what was the intent of such advertisements/films as "Birth of a nation", "The eternal Jew" or "The last temptation of Christ"? Did those expressions intend to misinform, inform, insult or incite and whom did they intend to misinform, inform, insult or incite?

And what were the reactions and consequences to such advertisements/films and by whom?

The film also creates an atmosphere of opportunity for many Muslims to determine whether their reactions are to the visual depiction or to the dogmatic dialogue in the film.

If the source of the visual depiction is imagination, mischief or malevolence based on bigotry and hatred which is embraced as freedom of expression by many, then is the reaction justifiable or misguided?

If the source of the dialogue is the sunna-hadiths (i.e. al Hajjaj's vol 2, pg 285 reference to child brides) which are embraced as religious dogma by many Muslims, then is the reaction justifiable or misguided?

Just as the film allows bigots to ponder the responsibilities and consequences that accompany freedom of expression, hopefully adherents of the sunna-hadiths will ponder the rationality and consequences that accompany freedom of reaction.

Perhaps it is time for many Muslims to consider whether a lot of the hearsay, gossip, rumor and slander regurgitated in the so-called sunna-hadiths are actually more blasphemous, dishonorable, defaming and insulting than any bigoted film, cartoon, advertisement, legislation, speech or sermon.

Beware of the preachers, producers, politicians, publishers and protesters who seek to prevent the unity of the Family of Abraham and mislead many away from the wisdom expressed in the Holy Quran (2:136).

Haram Branch, Mississippi

Letter # 74

<u>WOLVES IN SHEPHERD'S CLOTHING</u>

Peace and Goodwill, Family:

Concerning Mississippi's recent adoption of the Students Religious Liberties Act, I wonder whose words and authority the schoolchildren of Mississippi should heed when it comes to public prayers in school or at school activities?

Should Christian schoolchildren heed the words and whims of the Mississippi legislature, Governor Bryant, the Liberty Counsel and others or the words and wisdom of Christ as offered in the Gospel according to Matthew 6:5-8?

"And when you pray, you shall not be like the hypocrites are: for they love to pray standing in the synagogue (church) and on the corners of the street (in public), that they may be seen of men....... But you, when you pray, enter into your closet (privacy), and when you have shut the door (shut out distractions/vanities), pray to your Father (God).......
Therefore, do not be like them (hypocrites / narcissists / attention seekers), for your Father (God) knows what you **need** before you ask (pray)."

If Christians who heed the words and wisdom of Christ concerning prayer in public are recognized as being pro-Christ, should pseudo-Christians who ignore Christ and heed the words and whims of others concerning prayer in public be recognized as being anti-Christ?

Do pseudo-Christians display the mark of the beast on their head (in their thoughts) and on their hand (by their deeds) when they think, encourage and do that which is contrary to what they profess to be the teachings of Christ? (Apocalypse aka Revelation 13:16-18)

Being that other faiths do not forbid public prayer like Christianity does, what will be the reaction of Christian students, teachers, administrators and parents in Mississippi and elsewhere when a Muslim, Hindu, Jewish, Buddhist, Agnostic, Wiccan, Atheist or Satanist student seeks to offer prayers at ballgames, graduations or other events?

It may behoove the Mississippi legislature, Governor the Liberty Counsel and others in the so-called "Bible Belt"/Bigot Belt to heed the message in Matthew 18:1-14 as they encourage Christian children to pray in public and disobey Christ.

And if indeed the Student Religious Liberties Act isn't intended to proselytize but to offer religious liberties then why not legislate for Comparative Religion classes and perhaps offer students an opportunity to study such works as Thomas Paine's Age of Reason as they seek religious liberty?

Whether in Mississippi, Rome, Mecca, Jerusalem, Beijing, Lhasa, Calcutta, Lagos, Moscow or Washington D.C., I invite all to BEWARE of WOLVES in SHEPHERD'S CLOTHING!!!!!!!

Peace and Goodwill

                                                      Haram Branch, Mississippi

Letter # 75

20 Soil Seed 6B2020 (Mar 2013)

Go Forth!

Peace and Goodwill, Family

Entering a new season today, I do wish all the members in the Family in the Northern Hemisphere a blessed and rejuvenating season of Birthing.

If you were able to fulfill your First Day of Birthing Fast and took time to cleanse and renew yourself for the coming season(s) and year(s), may the benefits, blessings and consequences of your cleansing and renewal be evident to all in the Society of the Open Sky.

Whether in the Northern or Southern Hemisphere in the Society of the Open Sky I hope the new season will witness the next phase in the effort to sincerely and clearly accentuate the many Positive Commonalities within the Family of Abraham.

I invite all members of the Family to take a few moments to Read, Study and Contemplate the beautiful message offered in the nineteenth (19th) Chapter of the Book of Psalms and its magnificent testimony to the fact that throughout the Society of the Open Sky Creation is indeed the True Word of our Creator.

As we in the Northern Hemisphere complete our fast and begin the new season may our Creator guide and help us to Be a more loving and united Family as we this day go forth to Be for I AM's good.

The orders are issued, the door is opened and the path has been cleared to proceed into the next phase of removing the imposters and pretenders from their positions of misleadership.

Go forth in the name of our Creator and reclaim the Kingdom which awaits you and your descendants.

Let the new season be as a trumpet call rallying the warriors of I AM to assemble and march forth into the Glorious Battles ahead in the pursuit of the Peace and Goodwill which come only from I AM

Enjoy the victory!

In the Name of I AM

Haram Branch, Mississippi

Letter # 76

08 Tree 6B2021 (Dec 2014)

Do not confuse ISIL with Islam

It is quite obvious that in their vain attempt to slander Islam, certain media and individuals are eager to display their Islamphobia by propping up ISIL (Iblis' servants in Iraq and the Levant) as the image of Islam.

However, I am surprised the Sun Herald would slyly participate in such behavior by publishing such thinly veiled religious bigotry as the Dec. 8 column ("How the Islamic State drives Muslims from Islam") by Thomas Friedman of The New York Times.

Iblis is the Arabic word for the personification of evil (Satan). I share this linguistic lesson to distinguish between the Muslim majority and those who declare themselves to be ISIL. The Muslim majority considers ISIL and its financial, ideological, religious and sectarian supporters and/or sympathizers to be enemies of Islam.

In letters published by the Sun Herald years ago, I warned about the negative effects sunna-hadiths and sharia law have had and continue to have upon true Islam.

ISIL's apparent zeal to submit to sunna-hadiths and sharia law and the fact that the Sunni Council of Religious Scholars in Saudi Arabia gave ISIL its stamp of approval in this past summer bear witness to the relevancy of my warnings.

Just as it would be wickedly absurd to put cologne or perfume on a rose to enhance its fragrance, it is equally absurd to attach sunna-hadiths, sharia law or blatant bigotry to the beauty and fragrance of Islam.

The fact that out of the 1.5 billion Muslims on Earth only a few thousand misbelievers have joined the servants of Iblis or left Islam because of ISIL should shed light on the true motives and integrity of those who seek to use ISIL as their masterpiece of anti-Islamic propaganda.

Haram Branch, Mississippi

Letter # 77

18 Fire 6B2022 (Jan 2015)

Is the pen mightier than the sword?

The recent events at the offices of Charlie Hebdo in Paris may cause one to ponder whether "the pen is mightier than the sword."

After all, does history teach us that the pen of Thomas Paine or Thomas Jefferson was mightier than the sword of Crispus Attucks or General Washington in determining the outcome of the Revolutionary War?

Was the pen of William Garrison, Harriet Stowe or Abraham Lincoln mightier than the sword of Nat Turner, John Brown or General Grant in determining the outcome of the Emancipation War?

Were the pens of propagandists, politicians or publishers mightier than the swords of Field Marshal Zhukov, General Eisenhower, the Resistance or Robert Oppenhiemer in determining the outcome of World War II?

Were the pens of the apostles (Matthew 6:24) mightier than the swords of the conquistadors, crusaders, cavalry, capitalists or communists in determining the outcome of European aggression and expansionism?

Was the pen of the Prophet (Quran 96:4-5) mightier than the sword of the Commander-of-the-Faithful in determining the outcome of Abrahamic monotheism?

However, simultaneously one cannot dismiss the possibility that the pen is indeed mightier than the sword in its versatility to heal or harm, to ridicule or respect, to inform or misinform, to incite or console, to entice or prohibit, to provoke or prevent, to inspire or discourage, to stifle or share knowledge, to spread truths or lies or to promote peace or war.

Is the pen mightier than the sword or are they both handy tools in humanity's efforts to prevent or promote ill will, goodwill, war or peace?

Haram Branch, Mississippi

Letter # 78

20 Flower 6B2022 (May 2015)

Awaken and enjoy peace and goodwill

'Say you: We believe in God and the revelation given to us and to Abraham, Ishmael, Isaac, Jacob and their descendants and that given to Moses and Jesus and that given to all prophets sent from God. We make no difference between the prophets and we bow only to God in submission/obedience." (Quran 2:136)

As the enemies of Islam expose the extent of their misguidance by murdering, marching, plotting or preaching in response to duplicitous, disingenuous or disrespectful depictions of Prophet Muhammad, Believers who recognize the authenticity and wisdom of the verse above can't help but wonder why the same misguided ones do not react violently to depictions of Prophet Jesus, Prophet Moses or Prophet Abraham.

Those who bear witness that "there is no other God but God "and that creation is the quintessential messenger of God are comfortable in the reality that in the absence of contemporary photographs, portraits or depictions of the prophets then any current depictions of any prophet are acts of greed, fantasy, vanity or idolatry. We are also comfortable with the reality that such acts are subject to the natural consequences of truth and reason.

Those who "divide their religion into sects" (Quran 30:31-32) and idolize Prophet Muhammad have also declared any depiction of Muhammad is blasphemy. Such declarations are either a flawed understanding of the definition of blasphemy or a blatant display of idolatry.

Humanity's gradual emergence from the baptismal fires of the Soul War will hopefully allow many to awaken, arise and enjoy the peace and goodwill which flow between the seven Cs: Creator, creation, conscience, coexistence, consequences, common sense, common interests.

Haram Branch, Mississippi

Letter # 79

Trickle-down theory corrupts the system

Declaring "Politicians pervert the trickle-down theory," a recent letter, seems to ignore the possibility that the trickle-down theory perverts/corrupts politicians and has hindered government of, for and by the people while enhancing government of, for and by the corporations.

The drastic disparity in the accumulation of capital, which has increased in America and the world since 1980, is the best evidence that the trickle-down theory is as preposterous and specious today as it was during slavery, feudalism, pre-regulated capitalism, over-regulated socialism and the hocus-pocus redistribution of wealth to the wealthy by the so-called Great Society and Rea ganomics.

The trickle-down theory ignores the historical evidence that the mentality/spirituality of many humans will guide them to selfishly and greedily accumulate, hoard and control the circulation of capital and impede the "pursuit of happiness," thus undermining the unselfish and healthy circulation of capital and opportunity.

Imagine capital and opportunity being to an economic system what blood and oxygen is to a biological system.

Imagine what the prognosis for any biological or economic system will be if 90 percent of the blood and oxygen or the capital and opportunity accumulates and remains in only 10 percent of the circulatory system.

Is the mentality and spirituality of humanity guiding it to ignore or heed the symptoms and warning signs of an impending consumer embolism, capital infarction, free-market stroke or socioeconomic paralysis?

Haram Branch, Mississippi

Letter # 80

9 Tree 6B2022 (Dec 2015)

Irresponsible Journalism

To the Editor:

The mantra "see something, say something" apparently does not apply to the publisher and editors of the Sun Herald, considering their decision to see and say nothing about the blatant religious bigotry and irresponsible journalism displayed by their reporter in the December 6, 2015, article on page 10A.

In paragraph seven of the article the reporter states definitively and without source, except the misinformation of a career Islamophobe, that "he cited several places that proved Allah is Satan". Such a bias and opinionated statement by a journalist should not have gotten to print unless there was unprofessional negligence or deliberate duplicity by the editors.

After all, at this point in the information age and fourteen years after 9-11 Americans who are not distracted or possessed by bigotry, hatred, fear, arrogance or ignorance understand that Allah is merely the Afro-Arabic word for God in the same sense that Dios is the Latino-Spanish word for God or in the same sense that a particular word in any other language is used to refer to the one and only Infinite-yet-Obvious Creator and Sustainer.

Actually, the theological debate (discussion) has been and will be whether "Jesus is God" and whether Muslims, Jews, Jehovah Witnesses, Unitarian Christians, Unibaptist Christians, Adam, Eve, Akhenaton, Nefertiti, Abraham, Hagar, Sarah, Moses, Mary, John, Jesus, Muhammad and other monotheists are in error because we do not believe "Jesus is God".

While a simple Google search will reveal that the meaning or translation of the word "Allah" is not really open for debate, a sincere scriptural search will reveal that the many examples of Jesus worshipping God (Matthew 6:9-13),

Jesus obeying God (John 5:30 or 7:16-19), Jesus loving God (Mark 12:29-30), Jesus glorifying God (John 12:28-33), and Jesus observing the Creation (Word) of God (Matthew 6:24-32) may indeed leave the doctrine (Matthew 15:9) that says "Jesus is God" open for debate (John 20:17).

Haram Branch, Mississippi

Letter # 81

5 Wind 6B2023 (Feb 2016)

Bigot Bait and Xenophobia

Dear Editor;

While it is apparent that not all of Trump's supporters are bigots, it is also apparent that his message has proven to be effective bigot bait.

It is undeniable that Trump's rhetoric is an appetizing lure to attract those who choose to embrace their racial, religious, gender or nationalist bigotry.

Seeking to "make America great again" like it was back when most of America preferred bigotry over liberty, many Trump supporters, refusing to adapt to America's metamorphosis, have chosen to ignore America's progressive path to equal rights, globalism and ideological/political evolution. Instead they desire to detour onto the regressive path to ideological/political obsolescence, isolationist nationalism and situational rights.

Whether it is an idea, individual, party, nation, economy, belief, religion or ideology, that which fails to adapt to the evolutionary direction which its environment presents is doomed to malfunction, dysfunction or inevitable extinction.

I invite voters to review the partisan platforms and assess whether they appeal to the bigoted interest of your race, religion, gender, party or nationalism or to the best interest of your family, your principles and your humanity.

America is approaching a fork in the road of history and November's presidential and legislative elections will determine whether America becomes "great again" like back when or America becomes greater than it is or has been.

Haram Branch, Mississippi

Letter # **82**

LAPTOPS Political Platform

Life

Ancestors

Posterity

Truth

Opportunity

Preamble

Seven Cs

The seven Platforms of Consideration listed above may be considered if the need arises to have a basis for future political activities with the objective of forming "a more perfect union" of the human experience in order to promote social justice and spiritual enhancement.

Life: Political activities should recognize, respect and promote the sanctity of Life.

Ancestors: Political activities should recognize, reflect and promote the life-enhancing hopes, efforts and accomplishments of our Ancestors.

Posterity: Political activities should recognize, respect and promote the life-enhancing hopes, efforts, accomplishments and potential of our Posterity.

Truth: Political activities should recognize, respect and promote the life-enhancing application of Truth in the pursuit of justice, commerce, knowledge and integrity.

Opportunity: Political activities should recognize, respect and promote the life-enhancing pursuit of individuals, families and other social units to enjoy, enhance and share their natural birthright to the Opportunity to be alive, productive and happy.

Preamble: Political activities should recognize, respect and promote the life-enhancing ideology, objectives and principles prescribed in the Preamble to the U.S.A. Constitution.

Seven Cs: Political activities should recognize, respect and promote the life-enhancing relationship between the Seven Cs [Creator, creation, conscience, consequences, coexistence, common sense and common interests]

DOMESTIC POLICY

Domestic policies, based on consideration of LAPTOPS, should focus on the following:

1. SECURITY against domestic and foreign threats to the implementation of LAPTOPS and allotting land (1 acre for every two years of service) to veterans or their immediate family, if veteran is deceased.

2. BUDGET designed to alleviate the burden of debt on Posterity by implementing:

   (a) a seven-year plan for taxation at 1957 rates to pay debt and spending at 1977 rate for infrastructure, security and poverty and then establishing a fair flat tax rate of 10% on income over $40k and 10% on sales (except food, water, medicine/healthcare) and elimination of all tax loopholes.

   (b) a process wherein the taxpayers (after the 7 year plan) can designate whether all or a percentage of their taxes should be used to fund either security, infrastructure, emergency/foreign aid, education/research, environment/exploration, poverty or administration

   (c) a retroactive confiscation of ill-gained profits made by political, media and military industrial profiteers from the wars/conflicts since 2001 to be used to help veterans and civilian victims of such wars/conflicts

   (d) a percentile based spending plan wherein, except during warfare or emergency, 15% of taxes is allotted for security, 10% for administration, 20% for infrastructure/environment, 10% for emergency/foreign aid, 15% for education/research, 15% for poverty, 15% for healthcare/exploration

   (e) a strict enforcement of harsh penalties for tax evasion, fraud, waste, abuse, theft, political/financial corruption, overpriced healthcare/insurance and illegal hiring practices

(f) a balanced budget amendment with safeguards for war and emergency

(g) an amendment for the establishment of an Economic Branch of government wherein qualified nonpartisan economists, one per state, are elected for 6 year term to advise the Executive, the Legislature and the People and recommend a sound short-term (1 to 5 years), mid-term (5 to 10 years) and long-term (10+ years) economic policy

3. JUSTICE based on equal protection and treatment under civil, commercial, criminal and constitutional law with emphasis on:

(a) the removal of any appearance of a double/triple standard

(b) the removal of all immunity from prosecution of government officials

(c) reexamination of the cost and effectiveness of the private prison industry

(d) reexamination of the cost and quality of legal representation as it relates to socioeconomic status

(e) enacting and enforcing harsher penalties for crimes against children, elders, and disabled individuals and for invasion of privacy, slander (through social media or otherwise) and the hiring of illegal immigrants while decriminalizing personal behaviors which do not harm others or impede upon public safety

(f) allowing victims/victims' families a greater role in determining penalties and minimizing the People's obligation to provide anything other than shelter, hygiene and nutrition to prisoners while maximizing the prisoner's family, religious affiliates or charities obligation to provide all else

(g) reexamine the necessity of establishing a precedent for Posterity by prosecuting political, military, media and intelligence officials for war crimes committed since August 7, 1979

4. ENVIRONMENT should be safeguarded by enacting and enforcing harsher penalties for polluting and endangering the quality of life and

experience of Posterity to enjoy nature's beauty and bounty. Implement a program wherein children 0-17 are allowed an opportunity to spend 1 week a year in nature as part of their scholastic curriculum

5. EDUCATION reform should be based on reassessment of cost vs benefit of post high school academia as well as reexamination of various methods to obtain accredited post high school degrees, certificates or licenses other than the current methods of academia and accreditation

6. POLITICAL reform should be implemented by:

   (a) moving more toward direct democracy wherein the People, as technology allows, through referendum, has a greater role in repealing and enacting legislation while retaining elected representatives to serve on necessary committees and to legislate when technology is inadequate to accommodate direct representation.

   (b) realizing that until a more progressive form of direct representation is implemented all efforts should be made to repeal or overturn any legislation or ruling which allows the misrepresentative influence of special interest money to have greater sway in political matters than the representative influence of the common interest of the People

   (c) enacting legislation that requires the participation of at least 60% of eligible voters to validate any election or referendum

   (d) enacting and enforcing harsher penalties for political corruption and misconduct

7. HEALTHCARE reform should be based on a reassessment of the cost of long and short-term healthcare, the cost and coverage of all insurance, the cost and effectiveness of medication and whether the People, religious organizations, charities or philanthropy are obligated to contribute to causation-determinative healthcare for the poor and elderly and universal healthcare for children and the disabled.

FOREIGN POLICY

Foreign policies, based on consideration of LAPTOPS, should focus on the following:

1. HUMAN RIGHTS within any nation we are involved with should be equal to or surpass the Human rights we cherish as a People and all nations we are involved with should recognize, respect and refrain from threatening the implementation of LAPTOPS and our overall Security.

2. COMMERCE with any nation we are involved with should be equitable and in the best interest of the People of that nation and our nation. We, the People, while seeking to achieve a more proportionate wage to profit/wage to pricing ratio domestically, must also recognize the irreversible trend toward a global economy and should prepare accordingly for ourselves and our Posterity.

3. When interacting with other nations HUMAN RIGHTS must supersede COMMERCE and our closest allies and associates should be those whose domestic and foreign policies recognize, respect and promote the life-enhancing principles of the LAPTOPS political platform

Society of the Open Sky
Ancient Garden of Prayer
Haram Branch, Mississippi
USA, ISA

Letter # **83**

Family of Abraham Mission

Peace and Goodwill

You are hereby invited to be a part of the pioneer generation in the establishment, growth and mission of the Family of Abraham Mission.

Awaken, arise and bear witness, with all of Creation, to the purification and rebirth of the genuine Family of Abraham.

Please take time to consider the Bylaws of the Family of Abraham Mission and determine whether the Bylaws identify you as a genuine member of the Family of Abraham.

The days of waiting, wondering and wandering are over. The spiritual harvest is ripe and the call is now being sent forth on this day to identify the genuine Family of Abraham so we may fulfill our destiny as the gleaners and gatherers of the fruits of the spiritual harvest, God willing.

If the Mission Statement/Bylaws of the Family of Abraham Mission identify you as a genuine member of the Family of Abraham, please seek guidance from our Creator and "be".

Enjoy the purification, rebirth, peace and goodwill offered by our Creator.

May our Creator guide and bless the Family of Abraham Mission in the days and years to come.

Peace and Goodwill

Family Of Abraham Mission

MISSION STATEMENT & BYLAWS

Mission Statement

In the name of I AM, we seek to promote social
justice and spiritual enhancement.

Bylaw I. Method

We seek to promote social justice and spiritual enhancement by sincerely.

Proclaiming: There is no other god but God; the Indivisible, Obvious and Infinite One.

Proclaiming: Creation is the original, natural Messenger and Word of God.

Proclaiming: Submitting to the Word of God and treating others as I want to be treated is the original, natural Way to obey God.

Obligating oneself to volunteer or donate to help those who need assistance.

Obligating oneself to understand and agree to the Statements of Belief, Commitment and Respect.

Obligating oneself to Pray/Meditate regularly and maintain a Family Tree and Journal.

Obligating oneself to Read/Study the message unveiled in the little book Seventh Apocalypse.

Bylaw II: Statement of Belief

We believe in One, Indivisible, Obvious and Infinite God.

We believe Creation is the original, natural Messenger and Word of God.

We believe submitting to the Word of God and treating others as we want to be treated is the original, natural Way to obey God.

We believe any scriptural verse, legislative law, theology, tradition, theory, theorem, religion, government, belief, ideology, policy, action, commentary or saying which disobeys, undignifies, distorts, profanes, pollutes or contradicts the original Way and Word of God should be exposed, resisted and rejected.

We believe God has entrusted Humans with the ability to affect the expansion of the Way and the Word whenever Humans obey the Way and Word, experience and share happiness, express positive prayers, meditations or praise and enjoy and share the Divine gifts of freedom, truth, justice, hope, compassion, love and life.

We believe the Poems, Letters, Recommendations and Warnings to repent and renew that are shared in the book Seventh Apocalypse are intended to clarify the Way and the Word.

We believe the duty of the FAMILY of ABRAHAM MISSION is to obey the Way and Word of God and invite everyone to repent, renew and obey the original Way and Word of God and enjoy the seven Divine Gifts in order to promote social justice and spiritual enhancement.

Bylaw III: Statement of Commitment

We commit ourselves to be obedient to the Way and Word of God.

We commit ourselves to be good and to reject evil.

We commit ourselves to be active in relieving suffering, being kind and being healthy.

We commit ourselves to be a productive, positive influence on society; especially for children.

We commit ourselves to prevent and defend against ignorance, aggression and oppression.

We commit ourselves to be active in promoting social justice and spiritual enhancement.

We commit ourselves to be consistently observant of the Proclamations, Statements and Obligations of the Family and the message of Seventh Apocalypse.

Bylaw IV: Statement of Respect

We recognize and respect the rights, dignity and life of all Humans and the laws of any society which recognizes and respects the rights, dignity and life of Humans.

We recognize and respect the rights, purpose and existence of all aspects of Creation.

We recognize and respect the authentic monotheistic scriptures which reflect and agree with the original, natural Way and Word of God.

We recognize and respect the intentions of the Poems, Letters, Warnings and Recommendations offered in Seventh Apocalypse.

We recognize and respect the purpose and procedure of the weekly Assembly and Gathering and the annual Celebrations.

We recognize and respect the purpose and duties of the Administrators of the Family.

We recognize and respect the Proclamations, Statements and Obligations of the Family.

Bylaw V: Order of Gathering

Join and be active in existing political parties, organizations, charities and monotheistic Fellowships with the sincere intent to (a) offer praise and thanks to our Creator; (b) emit QYQNQYQ energy in order to remove evil and suffering and enhance happiness and healing;

(c) share the objectives of LAPTOPS and (d) promote social justice and spiritual enhancement.

Annual Celebrations

1) Fasting and Atonement Day- First day of Birthing (Spring); 24hr fast from all intake, dawn to dawn, as health permits.

2) Freedom and Family Day – 4th of Bird (July)

3) Feast and Thanksgiving Day – 4th Blackday (Thursday) in Fruit (November)

4) Ancestors and Posterity Day – 25th of Tree (December)

BYLAW VI: Duties of Administrators

The organization of a Family of Abraham Mission, whether
at the community, district, state, national, international
or interplanetary level should be as follows:

1) Moderator: a) guards the Bylaws, Property and Integrity of the Family; b) moderates Gatherings/Assemblies; c) in the presence of a Gathering and an Assembly, international Moderator anoints and community Moderator appoints succeeding Moderator(s) of one or three appointees upon accepting position as Moderator with the prerogative to replace, in the presence of a Gathering and an Assembly, the anointed or appointed as needed or preferred; d) preside at meetings and Judicial Proceedings; e) be Commander of the Pen, Sword and Peace; f) veto legislation or referendums; g) deliver message on Freedom and Family Day and Ancestors and Posterity Day.

Anointed at the international level and appointed at community level based on efforts to organize and is elected at the district, state, national and interplanetary levels according to Bylaw VII.

*Serve for lifetime except in case of incapacitation or violation of Bylaws.

2) Associate Moderator: a) assumes duties of absent Administrators as needed; b) as needed, organizes/supervises elections; c) with the Keeper of the Peace, monitors the duties of the Treasurer; assist Moderator in maintaining Properties

*Elected for two-year term.

3) Secretary: a) records and reports proceedings of meetings; b) assumes duties of Associate Moderator in case of absence, incapacitation or violations until election within thirty days; c) monitors elections.

*Elected for two-year term.

4) Treasurer: a) manages and reports income and expenditures; b) assumes duties of Secretary in case of incapacitation or violation until election within thirty days; c) with the Keeper of the Peace, screens and distributes requests for help.

*Elected for two-year term.

5) Keeper of the Peace: a) monitors unity among Members and conducts Public Relations in consultation with Moderator; b) assumes duties of Treasurer in case of incapacitation or violation until election; c) with Treasurer, screens and distributes requests for help; d) duties assumed by Moderator in case of incapacitation or violation until election within thirty days.

*Elected for two-year term.

6) Keeper of the Sword: a) administers security in consultation with Moderator; b) duties assumed by Moderator in case of incapacitation or violation until election within thirty days; c) represents Family in Judicial proceedings; d) liaison with other political, security entities.

*Elected for two-year term

7) Keeper of the Pen: a) supervises publication and education activities in consultation with the Moderator; b) duties assumed by Moderator in case of incapacitation or violation until election within thirty days; c) supervises Youth activities; d) liaison with academic, scientific and artistic entities; e) represents the accused at Judicial proceedings as needed.

*Elected for two-year term

Bylaw VII: Membership and Order of Procedure

MEMBERSHIP:

1) Membership is established by, if physically and/or mentally able, agreeing to the Mission Statement, proclaiming the Proclamations, understanding and accepting the Statements, vowing to fulfill the Obligations prescribed and abiding by the Bylaws of the Family of Abraham Mission. If an interested individual is physically or mentally unable to do the above he or she may establish membership if there is an individual who acts as their surrogate to agree, proclaim, understand, accept, vow and abide.

2) All Members are eligible for Nomination and Election to Administrative positions.

3) All Members are encouraged to volunteer for non-Administrative positions.

ORDER OF PROCEDURE:

1) Members must be notified of Meetings at least 48 hours prior (except in an emergency) and meetings can proceed only with a quorum of four (4) Administrators and one-third (1/3) of Membership and must observe agreed-on Rules of Order.

2) All elections, actions and referendums are decided by a majority of Members and require the participation of at least 50% of the Membership utilizing the principle of one-person, one-vote.

3) One copy of minutes and reports are to be made available to Members upon request.

4) All affiliates must be approved by international Moderator and conform to the Bylaws.

5) All accusations of violating the Bylaws are subject to judicial proceedings with witnesses and will be adjudicated by a jury of seven Members or by presiding Moderator, as the accused chooses.

6) The penalty for violations, whether in the form of an apology, a fine, service to victim, suspension of membership or banishment from the Family, will be decided by the presiding Moderator and all verdicts and penalties may be appealed once before a full body of the (7) Administrators at the next two higher levels for a majority ruling.

7) Vetoes may be overridden by a majority of Administrators and three-fifths (3/5) of the general Membership of the particular Mission level and the same method is used to recall elected Administrators or amend Bylaw VII.

May our Creator guide and bless the Family of Abraham Mission as we enjoy the purification, rebirth, peace and goodwill offered by our Creator.

Society of the Open Sky
Ancient Garden of Prayer
Haram Branch, Mississippi
USA, ISA

Letter # 84

4 Bird 6B2023 (July 2016)

Invitation to prepare for the Islamic
States of the Americas (ISA)

Intending to promote social justice and spiritual enhancement, I greet you with peace and goodwill as a fellow Miracle of God (Exodus 3:14-15; John 7:16-17; Quran 96:1-8; Book of Creation 1:1).

I bear witness that there is no other god but God, the Creator and Sustainer.

I bear witness that Creation is the first and final messenger of God.

I bear witness that the Quran and Bible, as they reflect and respect the universal, divine message of the Holy Book of Creation, are messages of wisdom and guidance offered to humanity as a gift from the grace of God.

I bear witness that peace and goodwill among humans is possible when humans choose not to hinder but to enjoy and enhance the Divine Birthright to life, freedom, hope, justice, compassion, truth and love.

Intending to promote social justice and spiritual enhancement, I invite all to prepare for the coming of ISA (the Islamic States of the Americas)

While considering this invitation to prepare for the Islamic States of the Americas (aka, Amiracle; aka Atchyzlan / 30 to 180 degrees West), the People of the western hemisphere will hopefully recognize our historical, current and future role in the metamorphosis of the Islamic States of the Americas.

Islam (obedience or submission to the will of God as revealed and proclaimed by the divine laws, lessons, instincts, intuitions, structures, sciences, facts, reason, revelations, reality and rhythms of Creation and by the sacred experiences of life, love, compassion, hope, truth, justice and freedom) is the fastest growing monotheistic identity in the western hemisphere and is on the trajectory to eventually be the chosen spiritual identity of most of the People in the western hemisphere who sincerely seek to be in harmony with the will of our Creator.

The history of the development of the existing civilization within the territory known as the Americas or the western hemisphere bears witness that the foundation for a society based on Islam, as defined above, has been deeply, solidly and firmly lain and is now being prepared for further construction.

Close examination of the traditions, beliefs and behavior of most inhabitants and institutions of the Americas will reveal that indeed the Americas may be the most Islamic society in the world today.

Although many in America may describe their spiritual identity as being Judeo-Christian, closer scrutiny of traditions, beliefs and behavior reveals that whether the issues are individualism, family, community, knowledge, warfare, resistance, economics, divorce, freedom of religion, modesty, health, democratic governance, taxation, charity, fasting, prayer or monotheism, most societal statutes and individual values in America actually reflect the fundamental tenets of genuine Islam more than the fundamental tenets of Judeo-Talmudom, Euro-Christendom or Arabo-Shariadom.

For instance, although according to Matthew 6:1-34 Jesus specifically instructed his disciples to obey/submit to the Islamic principles of monotheism, prayer, charity, fasting and freedom, most inhabitants of the Americas reject the Gospel according to Matthew 5:39-44 that says Christians should "not resist evil" and instead most inhabitants of the West choose to embrace the Islamic principle of resisting evil, aggression, oppression, criminality, injustice, arrogance, ignorance, hypocrisy and hatred.

Whether out of hypocrisy, ignorance or apostasy most people within the Americas who claim to be Christians also ignore the Biblical teachings to "turn the other cheek", "love your enemy", "give no thought for tomorrow", "be obedient to your slave-masters", "be submissive to your husbands" and to refrain from divorce, polygamy, sex outside of marriage and killing human beings.

After all, is it hypocrisy or apostasy for an individual to claim to be a Christian and to love his or her enemy and yet serve in the military or any security apparatus with the intention to indiscriminately and unquestionably kill another human being just because someone or some government orders him or her or allows him or her to kill another human being as a matter of "duty"?

What would the Biblical Jesus do?

What would the Quranic Jesus do?

While apparently reflecting and respecting most of the natural, social and spiritual principles of genuine Islam, simultaneously many in the West are increasingly rejecting Judeo-Talmudom's and Euro-Christendom's key doctrines of religious dogma.

Most Jews are reexamining and rejecting such theological doctrines as a "chosen" people, "holy" real estate, ecumenical Talmudism, ritual mutilation, the exaltation of rabbinicism, the idolizing of Zionism and the infallibility of the Torah.

Also, most Christians are reexamining and rejecting such theological doctrines as "original sin", human sacrifice for the redemption of sin, intercessional prayer, ecumenical Paulism, the exaltation of priest-craft, the idolizing of Jesus or saints and the infallibility of the Bible.

Likewise, while respecting the universal principles of Islam, most Muslims, heeding the Quran's instructions that Believers and Behavers should "make no difference between one and another" of the Prophets (2:133-136), that there should "be no compulsion in religion" (2:256) and that Believers must not "divide into mere sects" (30:31-32), are increasingly rejecting Arabo-Shariadom's key doctrines of religious dogma.

Most Muslims, especially since the appearance of Iblis' Servants in Iraq and the Levant (ISIL), are reexamining and rejecting Shariadom's theological doctrines of Arab sunna-hadithism, cultural sexism, "sacred" real estate, fratricidal sectarianism, religious compulsion and intolerance, the exaltation of religious clerics, the idolizing of Muhammad and the infallibility of the Quran or other religious writings.

While recognizing and adhering to the life-enhancing, universal and monotheistic message of religious books and rejecting the life-threatening, sectarian and polytheistic message of religious books, most monotheistic inhabitants of the western hemisphere realize that all books are susceptible to editing, forgery, embellishment, mistranslation, misinterpretation or destruction by the minds and hands of humans. Realizing this reality most people in America and beyond stand united in the common struggle (jihad) to obey/submit to the will of God by simply living and promoting a lifestyle that does not hinder or harm but rather helps and enhances life, justice, hope, truth, compassion, love and freedom. All genuine Believers and Behavers share the common concept of submitting to God by simply believing that God is and by "doing unto others as you want done unto you".

This religious/spiritual reexamination and the gradual unveiling of America's true spiritual identity have been accelerated by the events which unfolded during the thirteen years before and after 9-11-2001 (6B2008). Despite the efforts of many in the media, military, madrassas, mosques, caliphates, churches, synagogues, legislatures, corporations, dictatorships, monarchies, theocracies and terrorist groups who have distorted or attempted to usurp the identity of Islam during this timeframe, it is Believers and Behavers living in the Americas who have preserved and guarded the identity of true Islam as forecasted in the Quran (47: 38).

Ironically, the events unfolding after 9-11 also continue to sufficiently expose the true identity of those who have geographically, historically and hypocritically claimed Islam as their spiritual identity yet slander and misrepresent Islam by their traditions, beliefs and behavior as they conveniently provide ample opportunities for objective observers to discern between Arabo-Shariadom and genuine Islam.

The events arising from 9-11 also continue to sufficiently expose those who hypocritically claim Judeo-Christianity as their spiritual identity yet slander and misrepresent Judaism and Christianity by their traditions, beliefs and behavior as they conveniently provide ample opportunities for objective observers to discern between Judeo-Talmudom or Euro-Christendom and genuine Judaism or genuine Christianity.

There is also irony in the fact that since 9-11 many truth-seekers in the Americas, especially citizens in the military, media, academia, clergy, political, justice and business sectors, have been introduced to Islam and provided a clearer understanding of and insight into Islam than they had prior to that pivotal morning. Among enlightened, unbigoted inhabitants of the western hemisphere, this introduction to and transparent scrutiny of Islam during the past thirteen years have progressively enhanced the understanding of the fundamental principles of true Islam while simultaneously exposing the sinister verses and blasphemous versions propagated and practiced by the current pseudo-Muslim enemies of Islam.

This clearer understanding of true Islam by many in the western hemisphere has awakened enlightened citizens to the realization that while many may identify themselves as Judeo-Christians it appears that based on belief and behavior America's true spiritual identity is more Islamic monotheism/deism than Judeo-Christendom polytheism, materialism, paganism, narcissism, celestialism or atheism.

Ancient, recent and modern history bears witness that all societies have embraced some form of religious or spiritual identity which inevitably has a significant effect upon the viability of the individuals, families, communities, government, ideology, culture, economy, ecology, health, mores and peace of that society.

Historically, the spiritual identity of most societies has been narcissism, paganism, celestialism, materialism, atheism, polytheism or monotheism.

Has the current society in the western hemisphere arrived at a point in its social, mental and spiritual evolution whereat it must now reassess its spiritual identity and determine which of the seven isms it will embrace as it adapts to the evolution of its individualism, information, science, technology, ideology, culture, politics, economy, ecology, social justice and spiritual enhancement?

Will the majority of the People in the western hemisphere embrace narcissism, paganism, celestialism, materialism, atheism, polytheism or monotheism as their spiritual identity in the days, years, decades and centuries to come?

Will the information/technology age, the disdain for hypocrisy, the entropy of western oligarcracy, the new archaeological/anthropological/cosmological/scientific discoveries, the current resurrection of Thomas Paine's "Age of Reason" and the inevitable implosion of Talmudom, Christendom and Shariadom create a spiritual identity vacuum in the lives of many in the western and eastern hemisphere?

If such a vacuum occurs and if "nature abhors a vacuum" and if it is written in the Holy Book of Creation that something will inevitably fill such a void, then which of the seven isms will fill the spiritual identity vacuum currently occurring in the western hemisphere?

If the society in the western hemisphere chooses monotheism to fill the spiritual identity vacuum will it be vigilant in distinguishing between genuine monotheism, tribal narcissism or theanthropic paganism?

If the Americas indeed chooses genuine monotheism as its spiritual identity and if, after the implosion of JudeoTalmudom, EuroChristendom and AraboShariadom, true Islam is recognized as the natural heir apparent to the concept of genuine monotheism, will genuine Islam fill the spiritual identity vacuum that is apparently occurring in the lives of many throughout the Earth?

Whichever ism is chosen to fill the spiritual identity vacuum in the days and years to come, will that choice naturally have a significant effect on the future development of all other aspects of society?

This invitation to prepare for the Islamic States of the Americas is offered based on the belief that historically every society has been and is built upon a particular spiritual identity which affects its viability and that civilizations have chosen either narcissism, paganism, celestialism, materialism, atheism, polytheism or monotheism as their spiritual identity. If this belief is factual, and if Islam, as defined herein, eventually proves to be the most viable monotheistic identity in the western hemisphere, then, God willing, this invitation to prepare will be worthy of consideration.

Seeking to promote social justice and spiritual enhancement, God willing, this invitation to prepare will fulfill its role of unveiling the cornerstone for the building of an Islamic society should the People of the western hemisphere choose monotheism as their spiritual identity.

After the impending economic, social, religious, political and cosmic upheavals and the removal of the impeding debris which has accumulated during the laying of the foundation for the Islamic States of the Americas, God willing, the People will see more clearly how to submit to the Master Architect, adhere to the Divine blueprint, utilize the cornerstone, choose the best building materials and harmoniously cooperate in the further construction and maintenance of the Islamic States of the Americas.

Awake, arise and prepare for the coming of ISA.

Society of the Open Sky
Ancient Garden of Prayer
Haram Branch
Mizisip, USA, ISA

Warning # 7

UNITY

Beware of the doctrine of the "trinity". It is a blasphemous, evil doctrine designed to defeat the mission of the true Christ and mislead and divide the Fellowship of Believers. Beware! (Matthew 7:21-23)

Will you believe the words delivered by Christ or the words fabricated by the Church - words which declare to children that Jesus is God (Exodus 20:7) even though Christ never claimed to be God (John 20:17).

It is time to come out of Babylon, where preachers, priests, teachers, nuns, theologians, profiteers, denominations, congregations and most citizens betray the true Christ yet offer sincere devotion to their creeds, theories, false faith and selfish fears or hopes. Those who worship the false Christ and betray the true Christ embrace their religion out of selfish fear of a punishment or in selfish hope of a reward.

Those who reject the false Christ and are brothers and sisters of the true Christ (Matthew 12:36-50) submit to the will of I AM the same way that the true Christ submitted to I AM - with love and obedience and not with fear of punishment or an expectation of reward, but simply because it is the right thing to do.

The followers of Saul Paul (1 Corinthians 11:1), the Nicene Creed of 325 c.e. and the evil theology of Trinitarian Christianity attempt to use the words at the end of the Gospel according to Matthew as evidence to support their twisted theory of the "trinity."

However I invite you to consider the following explanation of the "Great Commission".

Those who are or have been in the military will find it easy to relate to the "Great Commission" when it is seen as a chain of command with the purpose of accomplishing a mission.

When soldiers (disciples) are sent forth on a mission, they go in the name of Constitution (the Highest Authority or Father); in the name of the Order that has been issued (the Word or Son); and in the name of the Commander-in-Chief who issues the Order (the Revealer of the Word or Holy Spirit of Truth).

The Constitution, the Commander-in-Chief, the Order and the Soldier who carries out the Order are each separate units which come together in one Chain of Command in order to accomplish a mission. Although the Constitution, the Commander-in-Chief and the Order itself are all part of one Chain of Command, everyone realizes that each are distinct and that the Constitution is the Supreme Power to which the Commander-in-Chief and the Order are subservient. Neither the Commander-in-Chief or the Order is equal to or as powerful as the Constitution. On the contrary, the Commander-in-Chief and the Order and the Soldier are each servants of the Constitution and would never presume to act or be independent of the Constitution.

So it is with the relationship between the Creator, the Holy Spirit of Truth, the true Christ and the disciples of the true Christ.

If you are able to understand this analogy of a Chain of Command then you will see that it is treasonous to declare Jesus is equal to God or that Jesus is God.

If Christ says "my Father is greater than I" (John 14:28) and then says, "my Father and I are one" (John 10:30), is Christ contradicting himself or does he mean the love, will and purpose of his life is one in sync with the love, will and purpose of I AM? Shouldn't everyone in the Fellowship of Believers seek to submit to the purpose, will and love of I AM? (John 6:38; 8:58)

If the word "trinity" does not appear anywhere in the Gospel or Bible then where does such a concept originates?

If there is a sin which cannot be forgiven (Matthew 13:31-37), how will those people be judged who teach children that Jesus is God even though Christ very clearly teaches that he is not God but the messenger (Messiah) of God?

If a man or woman believes Jesus is God even though Christ says he is not God then is that woman or man following the desires of his or her own will, the will of Trinitarian Christianity or the will of the Anti-Christ?

If the concept of a "trinity" is obviously a lie (and we know who the father of all lies is) what is the ulterior motive of anyone who would invent such a lie about Christ or such a blasphemy against God?

If Christ says he is not God and ninety percent of those who say they are Christians believe Jesus is a god then who is that ninety percent being guided by –– who have they chosen to be their shepherd?

Hear the call of the Spirit of Truth (John 14: 15 - 31; Holy Quran 4: 171 and 19: 16 – 36) and repent and turn away from the evil doctrine of the "trinity" before it is too late.

You have been warned and will be judged by I AM.

Recommendation # 7

BAPTISM OF REPENTANCE AND REBIRTH

Anyone who chooses to genuinely renew the relationship of Being with I AM may perform the following Seven Steps of Initiation into a New Birth of Being:

1. During twenty-four hours of comfortable solitude with only pen, paper and weapon as amenities, beginning at dawn Initiates should fast from (a) all food, drink, smoke or any kind of intake, (b) all use of technology (except shelter), (c) all interaction with humans (unless assistance is needed due to disability), (d) all interaction with pets, (e) all reading material (except that written by the Initiate) and anything else that may interrupt the solitude.

   Or

   During forty-eight hours of comfortable solitude with only pen, paper and weapon as amenities and water and fruit as sustenance, beginning at dawn Initiates should fast during the forty-eight hours in the manner prescribed above.

2. The Initiate should begin the hours of solitude at sunrise by facing the seven directions of (1st) west, (2nd) south, (3rd) east, (4th) north, and again facing west, (5th) look downward, (6th) look upward and (7th) look inward and at each direction say aloud: "Thank you, I AM, for letting me Be."

3. During the hours of solitude the Initiate should perform Step (2) at least seven times and after each time ask I AM for healing, forgiveness and guidance seven times, as prescribed in Step (4).

4. The Initiate should seek healing, forgiveness and guidance by asking I AM (a) to heal all that the Initiate has harmed; (b) to heal and forgive the Ancestors and Descendants of the Initiate; (c) to heal

and forgive those whom the Initiate has influenced to commit harm; (d) to heal and help those who are suffering; (e) to heal and help the Innocent; (f) to heal the Initiate and forgive the Initiate for the harm the Initiate has caused to others or self; and (g) to guide the Initiate to be obedient to the will of I AM.

5. After completing Steps (2), (3) & (4) the Initiate should face the seven directions and at each direction thank I AM (a) for healing and forgiving; (b) for the guidance of I AM; and (c) for the gifts of freedom, justice, hope, compassion, truth, love and life.

6. The Initiate should complete the hours of solitude at dawn by facing the seven directions and at each direction saying aloud: "Thank you, I AM, for blessing me to Be one who will help and heal and will not hinder and harm."

7. Annually, except when at war or when ill, Initiates should complete the fast as prescribed at least once, if it is the will of I AM.

Poem # **15**

THE COVENANT

Sea to shining sea, the prophecy proceeds- old to new.
The drums gently echo a message of truth.
Sweet, soft, intensely harmonious, patiently slow,
The talking drums gently, sweetly echo.
Smoke signals rise quietly across the OPEN SKY.
Children dance, the land smiles and smoke signals explain why.

Across the wide, dear OPEN SKY blue
Smoke signals rise quietly, gently at noon----- a clue!
Five hundred years is the same as a half a day
As the descendants of slaves, natives and refugees live, dream and pray.
Listening to the rhythm of the drums, the People in unity dance
Vowing to give freedom, truth, reason, compassion and love a chance.

Rhythmic drums talk; ancient smoke signals upon the horizon are seen.
Five hundred years of sowing is ready to reap and glean.
Wheat and tares are gathered as the Children remember Exodus 3:14.
As Quran 3:52; 6:89; 57:28 and John 20:17; 7:16 and the Book of Creation
united speak
Drums and smoke signals from a baptizing fire shout to Humans
Who are Free:

I AM remembers the Covenant, Be!

Poem # 16

SUBMISSION

Enjoying the joy of the sound
Of the quiet, rhythmic breathing of a child
Sleeping, playing, praying, dancing, living, laughing and
Enjoying the blessings of life,
I hear I AM WHO I AM

Observing the metamorphosis and flutter of the butterfly
And the ripening upon the stem and stalk,
New moon to new moon,
Morning, evening, midnight to noon,
I see I AM WHO I AM

Awaiting the rise and fall of peoples and nations as each
Being blessed with choice, liberate or exploit
The innocence of Children and Creation
And ignore or prepare for the agony or splendor of a Promised Day,
I remember I AM WHO I AM

Respecting the act of judgment and its companion Justice
And the Truth and Love that are allied with Freedom
In the battle against the Wicked Three
Known as Blasphemy, Idolatry and Hypocrisy,
I know I AM WHO I AM

With my Life, Death and Life
And by the recognition of history and generations gone;
With my Life, Death and Life
And in the hope for Children today and Generations to come,
I submit to I AM WHO I AM.

Epilogue

Haram Branch, Mississippi

In the service, love, guidance and name of God (the Infinite-yet-Obvious One), may peace and goodwill be with us as we enjoy the seven gifts of freedom, truth, compassion, justice, hope, love and life and sincerely respect the laws and lessons of Creation.

Recent and current events bear witness that our Creator has placed the inhabitants of the Americas upon a new and unchartered path at this time is ourstory and if it is the will of the Most Gracious One the message of this little book may shed a light upon that path and help all involved to move forward into an inheritable tomorrow.

Being a free and simple man who has found it wise to glean the best from Creation and the monotheistic beliefs I have received from my Ancestors or encountered during my life, I have chosen to simply live as a Believer/Behaver in the Essence of the Infinite-yet-Obvious Reality that guides me to be able to enjoy and share the seven gifts.

It is from this viewpoint that I have written over the past forty years about the relationship between our Creator, Creation, the People of the Americas and the world, Judeo-Christianity and Islam. Developments arising from the convergence of the monotheistic faiths in the Americas during the past generation are a testament to the insight and foresight displayed in the letters, poems, warnings and recommendations compiled here.

This chronological collection of published letters to the editor and the accompanying opinions and observations are intended to promote understanding, reconciliation and healing as the People of the Americas and the world consider their monotheistic commonalities and differences in the days to come.

While the opinions and observations presented here may differ from some of the contemporary religious, political and economic ideologies embraced by most of the People of the Americas and the world, I feel confident that the People who seek peace and goodwill shall be able to recognize the relevancy of these letters and observations when viewed in the light of current and future events.

The title of this compilation is from a dream wherein the word "QYQNQYQ" (defined in the dream as that essence of spiritmatter which emanates from the positive intentions, thoughts, words and actions of humans and causes Creation to unveil, expand and transform in order to guide humanity to its best potential) appeared emblazoned upon the sky just before the sky opened. As the sky opened, the word "QYQNQYQ" was transformed or translated into the word "ESPYLACOPA" and appeared to be poured upon the Earth from the other side of the sky.

As a spiritual child of I AM I share these words at this time in the hope that it will be a reminder to all that the positive efforts and effects of People of peace and goodwill have natural consequences as we submit to the Way and Word of God, respect each others' birthright to the seven gifts and are vigilant in our personal contribution to the QYQNQYQ.

Bearing witness to the metamorphosis occurring within the relationship between our Creator, Creation and the People of the Americas and the world, perhaps these letters, warnings, recommendations and observations will be beneficial to the establishment of mutual respect, trust and common goals as humanity chooses the best path into the future; if it is the will of God.

Peace and Goodwill, in the love and guidance of I AM

Haram Branch, Mississippi, USA, ISA

Index

D

Deism 207

democracy 3, 72, 99, 100, 133, 135,
    136, 147, 148, 150, 153, 165, 193

dialogue 30, 76, 88, 91, 101, 174

Dietary 25, 34, 110, 169

differences 42, 87, 88, 107, 184,
    205, 217

direct democracy 193

direct representation 135, 136, 140,
    147, 148, 193

disciple of Christ 35

dogma xv, 23, 57, 60, 70, 154,
    174, 205

dreadlocks 2

dreams 32, 112, 114, 126, 133, 150,
    151, 157, 158, 215, 218

drums 130, 147, 171, 215

E

Earth 8, 10, 114, 171, 181, 208, 218

Easter 6

education 25, 140, 191, 193, 201

electric slide 84

Emerald Mound 98, 114

environment 26, 79, 140, 156, 157,
    161, 188, 191, 192

ESPYLACOPA 218

Europeanization 116

Exorcism 163, 164

F

false 5, 8, 12, 32, 55, 163, 210

Family 13, 20, 44, 52, 58, 82, 85, 90,
    108, 125, 163, 169, 175, 176,
    178, 188, 190, 191, 192, 195,
    196, 197, 198, 199, 200, 201,
    202, 204, 207

Family of Abraham 175, 178, 195, 196,
    197, 199, 201, 202

Family of Abraham Mission 195, 196,
    197, 199, 201, 202

fasting xiii, 13, 20, 42, 199, 204

fight 4, 22, 38, 44, 62

flag 3, 44, 45, 46, 49, 68, 95, 123, 124

foundation 15, 16, 20, 30, 50, 91, 103,
    144, 204, 208

freedom xiii, xiv, 3, 11, 16, 17, 19, 22,
    23, 25, 26, 29, 32, 34, 35, 36,
    38, 39, 43, 57, 60, 61, 62, 63,
    64, 66, 68, 70, 71, 72, 73, 74,
    75, 76, 78, 81, 82, 85, 88, 91,
    99, 100, 102, 104, 108, 114, 116,
    119, 120, 124, 127, 130, 138,
    140, 144, 152, 153, 156, 164,
    165, 168, 169, 170, 174, 175,
    197, 199, 203, 204, 206, 214,
    215, 216, 217

future xv, 6, 36, 40, 41, 43, 89, 96,
    106, 115, 119, 124, 129, 130,
    139, 149, 162, 163, 166, 189,
    203, 208, 218

G

garden 34, 194, 202, 209

garden of Gethsemane 34

Garden of Prayer 194, 202, 209

Gathering 110, 114, 133, 171, 198, 199

Gettysburg Address 120, 126

gifts xiv, 20, 26, 42, 57, 141, 197, 203,
    214, 217, 218

God xiii, xiv, xvii, 2, 3, 4, 6, 11, 17, 19,
    20, 21, 22, 23, 34, 35, 37, 42,
    48, 49, 53, 54, 57, 58, 59, 60,
    62, 67, 68, 70, 72, 75, 82, 86,
    87, 88, 91, 92, 95, 97, 104, 108,
    115, 138, 154, 163, 164, 172,

www.ingramcontent.com/pod-product-compliance
Lightning Source LLC
Chambersburg PA
CBHW030427290526
45786CB00001B/176